Corporate Acquisitions and Mergers in South Africa

Corporate Acquisitions and Mergers in South Africa

Second Edition

Yaniv Kleitman

Cliffe Dekker Hofmeyr Inc

This book was originally published as a chapter in Corporate Acquisitions and Mergers.

General Editor: Peter Begg

Wolters Kluwer

Published by:
Kluwer Law International B.V.
PO Box 316
2400 AH Alphen aan den Rijn
The Netherlands
E-mail: lrs-sales@wolterskluwer.com
Website: www.wolterskluwer.com/en/solutions/kluwerlawinternational

Sold and distributed by:
Wolters Kluwer Legal & Regulatory U.S.
920 Links Avenue
Landisville, PA 17538
United States of America
E-mail: customer.service@wolterskluwer.com

ISBN 978-94-035-2598-3

e-Book: ISBN 978-94-035-2608-9
web-PDF: ISBN 978-94-035-2618-8

Contents

Cliffe Dekker Hofmeyr Inc.

Cliffe Dekker Hofmeyr is one of the largest business law firms in South Africa with approximately 110 directors/partners and 350 qualified lawyers, located at offices in Johannesburg and Cape Town.

Cliffe Dekker Hofmeyr lawyers specialize in services covering the complete spectrum of business legal needs in our core practice areas.

Tel.: +27 11 562 1000

Fax: +27 11 562 1111

Website: www.cliffedekkerhofmeyr.com

1 GOVERNMENT, STRUCTURES AND CONSTITUTIONAL FRAMEWORK

[01] The Republic of South Africa is a constitutional democracy. The national, provincial and local levels of government all have legislative and executive authorities in their own spheres and are defined in the Constitution of the Republic of South Africa, 1996 as 'distinctive, interdependent and interrelated'. Operating at both national and provincial levels are advisory bodies drawn from South Africa's traditional leaders. It is a stated intention in the Constitution that the country be run on a system of cooperative governance. South Africa is led by a President, chosen by the members of the National Assembly, which, together with the National Council of Provinces, make up the South African Parliament.

[02] Parliament is the legislative authority of the country empowered to make laws for the country in accordance with the Constitution. Parliament is bound by the Constitution and must act within its limits. The National Assembly is elected by the people of the country, the national age of suffrage being 18 years, and is tasked with electing the President, passing legislation, scrutinizing and overseeing executive action and providing a national forum for public consideration of issues. The number of National Assembly seats awarded to each political party is in proportion to the outcome of the national election, which is held every five years.

[03] The National Council of Provinces fulfils the function of representing provincial interests in the national sphere of government. No bill that the National Assembly wishes to pass as legislation may be promulgated until it has been passed by the National Council of Provinces.

[04] The President, elected by the National Assembly from among its members, is the executive Head of State and leads the Cabinet. The President may not serve more than two five-year terms in office. The Cabinet consists of the President, the Deputy President and a number of Ministers. The President appoints the Deputy President and Cabinet Ministers. The Public Protector; the Human Rights Commission; the Commission for the Promotion and Protection of the Rights of Cultural, Religious and Linguistic Communities; the Commission for Gender Equality; the Auditor-General and the Independent Electoral Commission are governmental organizations that have been created to support constitutional democracy.

[05] Within the Constitution is a Bill of Rights applicable both to the state and to all persons in South Africa. The Bill of Rights is interpreted liberally by South Africa's courts with a strong emphasis placed on human rights. The fundamental rights contained within the Bill of Rights include the right to life, freedom of expression, free economic activity, freedom of association and religion, equality as well as the right not to be arbitrarily deprived of property. The rights contained within the Bill of Rights are subject to limitation only by a law of general application and to the extent that the limitation is reasonable and justifiable in an open and democratic society based on human dignity, equality and freedom and taking into account further factors such as the nature and purpose of the right.

2 LEGAL SYSTEM/COURTS

[06] The South African legal system is based on Roman-Dutch law, subject to the Constitution. However, the business and corporate laws of South Africa have a strong influence from English law and, to a lesser extent, the United States (US) law as well. Judicial authority is vested in the courts, which are established by, or pursuant to, the Constitution. The Constitutional Court is the highest court of the land in all matters. The Supreme Court of Appeal hears appeals from the various divisions of the High Court.

[07] The Constitutional Court exercises both exclusive and concurrent jurisdiction in constitutional matters. In respect of direct challenges to the constitutionality of all forms of legislation, concurrent jurisdiction is exercised between the Constitutional Court, the Supreme Court of Appeal and the High Courts. The Court of First Instance in such cases will, however, usually be the High Court.

[08] The Constitutional Court has exclusive jurisdiction to decide matters involving: disputes between organs of state concerning their constitutional status, powers or functions; the constitutionality of a parliamentary or provincial bill; a dispute over the constitutionality of an amendment to the Constitution; the question of whether Parliament or the President has failed to fulfil a constitutional obligation; and the certification of a provincial constitution. Decisions of the Constitutional Court are binding upon all persons and upon all legislative, executive and judicial organs of the state. Constitutional Court judges are appointed by the President in consultation with the Cabinet and on the recommendations of the Judicial Service Commission, an independent body. The Chief Justice and Deputy Chief Justice of the Constitutional Court are appointed by the President in consultation with the Judicial Service Commission. The leaders of parties represented in the National Assembly are also consulted in this regard.

[09] Judgments of the Supreme Court of Appeal are binding on all courts of a lower order, and judgments of the divisions of the High Court are binding upon the lower courts within their respective areas of jurisdiction. The Magistrates' Courts have both civil and criminal jurisdiction, and there are limits on the type of matters they can entertain as well as the monetary amount of these matters.

[10] Alternative methods of settling disputes also exist. The Arbitration Act 42 of 1965 governs the procedure to be followed in settling a matter through arbitration, which involves the determination of a dispute by one or more independent third parties rather than by a court.

[11] The King Report on Corporate Governance for South Africa, 2016 (King IV) also recommends that companies and other business entities take more concerted steps in seeking to resolve disputes via alternative dispute resolution (ADR) mechanisms such as arbitration and mediation. It states that ADR has been the most effective and efficient methodology to address the costly and time-consuming features associated with more formal litigation. Statistics related to success range from a low of 50% for those situations in which the courts have handed down a case for ADR to an average of 85%–90% where both parties are willing participants.

[12] ADR has thus become the intervention of choice in many instances, so it is appropriate for specialists to improve the overall rate of intake and success. Mediation is often more appropriate where the interests of the disputing parties need to be addressed and where commercial relationships need to be preserved and even enhanced. Mediation is often suggested as an ADR method with the assumption that the parties are willing to engage fully in the process. A process of screening is undertaken by many mediators, which excludes those who fall short of the criteria of will and capacity.

[13] Previously, King III recommended that in selecting a dispute resolution process, each case should be carefully considered on its merits and, at least, the following factors should be taken into account (these are not expressly set out in King IV, but in practice the same considerations continue to apply):

- Time available for the resolution of the dispute: Formal proceedings, and in particular court proceedings, often entail procedures lasting many years. By contrast, ADR methods and particularly mediation can be concluded within a limited period of time, sometimes within a day.
- Principle and precedent: Where the issue in dispute involves a matter of principle and where the company desires a resolution that will be binding in relation to similar disputes in the future, ADR may not be suitable. In such cases, court proceedings may be more appropriate.
- Business relationships: Litigation and processes involving an outcome imposed on both parties can destroy business relationships. By contrast, mediation, where the process is designed to produce a solution most satisfactory to both parties (a win-win resolution), may preserve relationships. Where relationships and particularly continuing business relationships are concerned, mediation or conciliation may be preferable.
- Expert recommendation: Where the parties wish to negotiate a settlement to their dispute but lack the technical or other expertise necessary to devise a solution, a recommendation from an expert who has assisted the parties in their negotiations may be appropriate. This process would be termed conciliation.
- Confidentiality: Private dispute resolution proceedings may be conducted in confidence. Further, the Arbitration Act makes provision for ADR processes to be conducted in private.
- Rights and interests. It is important, in selecting a dispute resolution process, to understand the fundamental differences between the various methods of dispute resolution (court proceedings, arbitration and adjudication). The adjudicative process involves the decision-maker imposing a resolution of the dispute on the parties after having considered the past conduct of the parties in relation to the legal principles and rights applicable to the dispute. This inevitably results in a narrow range of possible outcomes based on fundamental considerations of right and wrong. By contrast, mediation and conciliation allow the parties, in fashioning a settlement of their dispute, to consider their respective needs and interests, both current and future. Accordingly, where creative and forward-looking solutions are required in relation to a particular dispute and particularly where the dispute involves a

continuing relationship between the parties, mediation and conciliation are to be preferred. For example, a contract can be amended or materially rewritten.

[14] The lower civil courts consist of the Small Claims Courts and the Magistrates' Courts. The Small Claims Courts enjoy jurisdiction over claims, the value of which does not exceed South African Rand (ZAR)15 000. No legal representation is allowed, and juristic entities may not institute action in these courts although they may be sued there. The Small Claims Courts share territorial jurisdiction with the Magistrates' Courts.

[15] The Magistrates' Courts have jurisdiction over claims up to the value of ZAR400 000 (unless parties to an action agree otherwise) – the District courts are limited to claims up to ZAR200 000, and the Regional Courts are able to hear matters up to ZAR400 000, with some specific deviations from these general rules as indicated in section 29 of the Magistrates' Court Act 32 of 1944. The District Magistrates' Courts have no jurisdiction in matters where the status of a person is an issue, such as divorce or custody matters. Regional Magistrates' Courts have been granted the jurisdiction to hear suits relating to the nullity of a marriage or a civil union and relating to the divorce between persons (including those married in terms of customary law) and matters connected therewith. Claims exceeding ZAR400 000 may be instituted in the High Court of South Africa, which has a division in most of the country's major cities. Appeals from the Magistrates' Courts lie to the High Court. Appeals from the High Court are usually heard by a full bench of the particular division of the High Court that originally heard the matter. Appeals from the High Court lie to the Supreme Court of Appeal, which sits in Bloemfontein. Ultimately, the Constitutional Court may be the final Court of Appeal, either if the matter is a constitutional matter or where the Constitutional Court determines that the matter is one that raises an arguable point of law of general public importance which ought to be considered by it.

[16] The Constitutional Court, with its seat in Johannesburg, has jurisdiction over the entire Republic.

[17] Several special courts exist, which have the status of the High Court, such as Labour Courts, Land Claims Courts and Income Tax Courts. The Companies Act 71 of 2008 established the Companies Tribunal which has jurisdiction to rule on a number of (but not all) matters arising under the Companies Act, for example, relating to disputes around company name reservations and certain exemptions from the requirement to have social and ethics committees of the board.

[18] The criminal courts consist of the District and Regional Magistrates Courts and the High Court. Jurisdiction is divided on the basis of the nature of offences and the extent of the punishment that may be imposed. The hierarchy of appeal courts in criminal matters is virtually identical to the hierarchy of appeals in the civil courts.

[19] A prominent trend in business contracts, shareholders agreements and joint venture (JV) arrangements is to provide for various modes of ADR and deadlock-breaking mechanisms before there is resort to the civil courts.

3 ECONOMY AND INFRASTRUCTURE

[20] The country leads the continent in industrial output (an estimated 40% of Africa's total output) and mineral production (an estimated 45% of total mineral production) and generates most of Africa's electricity (over 60%). South Africa's economy is managed within a stable political environment. The current African National Congress government, which can broadly be described as socialist, has made a strong commitment to lowering inflation and reducing the fiscal deficit, which has had the effect of reducing South Africa's vulnerability to external pressures. The National Treasury has attempted to follow an economic strategy focused on growth and job creation. Poverty and unemployment remain as challenges to be overcome.

[21] The economy includes a modern financial and industrial sector supported by an established and continuously upgraded infrastructure. This modern aspect of the economy stands in contrast with a sizeable informal subsistence sector. South Africa's major strengths include its physical and economic infrastructures, natural mineral and metal resources, a growing manufacturing sector and the potential to develop a strong tourism industry. Trade and investment with other African states have increased substantially since the birth of the democratic era in 1994. The financial and industrial sectors are concentrated in the Gauteng province, which on its own accounts for about 34% of the country's gross domestic product (GDP). This is attributable to, among others, the fact that Gauteng is the most densely populated area in South Africa, accounting for about 23% of the country's population.

[22] Over the past five years, the pattern of GDP growth has been marked by strong performances in sectors with exposure to domestic demand, such as wholesale and retail trade, banking and financial services, real estate, transport and construction. Manufacturing growth slightly underperformed overall domestic growth over that period, while agricultural and mining displayed a greater degree of volatility.

[23] The country's bustling informal economy, largely unmeasured and unregulated, has developed alongside its sophisticated industrial economy and represents untapped potential for the country's future economic development. More particularly, strong growth in public sector capital spending and investment associated with the 2010 FIFA World Cup provided an important boost to the economy. The telecommunication sector has benefitted from significant capacity expansion in the past couple of years and is still growing. Several submarine cable systems have been launched in the last few years. These will increase the bandwidth available to several African countries including South Africa. The Eastern Africa Submarine Cable System, which will increase the bandwidth available to several African countries including South Africa, was completed in 2010. The West Africa Cable System, linking African countries between South Africa and the United Kingdom (UK), was launched in May 2012. The Africa Coast to Europe cable along the West African coast, linking South Africa and France, was completed in 2012. The Seacom undersea fibre-optic cable which links Southern and Eastern Africa went live in July 2009.

[24] Radio and television networks are highly developed with subscription satellite services in addition to public broadcasting networks available across the country. South Africa has a highly developed infrastructure of roads and rail links, as well as airports with commercial air travel to all major centres and airports and airfields in most towns. The Gautrain, a ZAR25 bn project of 80 km of rapid rail network, connects Johannesburg, Pretoria and OR Tambo International Airport.

[25] Being a dry country, South Africa has an impressive infrastructure of water storage dams, which include some hydroelectric installations. Electric power generation occurs through a national grid of power stations, with electricity being exported to neighbouring countries.

[26] The South African government has tried to meet many of its social service obligations, and much has been done to ensure that the constitutional right of every South African citizen to clean water is becoming a reality. The number of South Africans receiving social grants expanded to 19 m in 2023, providing an important safety net for low-income households. Of South Africa's over 13 m learners, more than 96% of children aged 4 to 18 are in school – a far higher enrolment rate than in most other developing countries.

[27] Housing is at the forefront of the national agenda for delivery, and the government is taking overall responsibility for providing houses to all. Again, the South African government has done much to realize the constitutional right of every South African citizen to access housing. Since 1994, the health sector has been radically transformed to give more access to the poor, improve quality and make the system more cost-effective. Free health services are now offered at public primary health care institutions. The current total health budget is approximately ZAR64 bn.

4 BLACK ECONOMIC EMPOWERMENT

[28] Transformation is a very important part of the South African legal and economic landscape. To this end, there are a number of legislative measures in South Africa aimed at promoting Black Economic Empowerment (BEE). Since South Africa became a democracy in 1994, a large number of corporate mergers and acquisitions have been concluded in the context of BEE, as large corporates (in particular listed entities) sought to improve and enhance their BEE ownership and standing. BEE deal activity is still prominent.

[29] Section 10 of the Broad-Based Black Economic Empowerment Act 53 of 2003 (BEE Act) compels organs of state and public entities to apply the BEE Codes of Good Practice (Codes), wherever reasonably possible, in:

- determining the qualification criteria for the issuing of licences, concessions or other authorizations in terms of any law;
- developing and implementing a preferential procurement policy;
- determining the qualification criteria for the sale of state-owned enterprises; and
- developing criteria for entering into partnerships with the private sector.

[30] While this provision is a mandatory obligation of the public sector (being specifically, a national or provincial department, municipality, Parliament, a constitutional institution and other public entities), it does have a strong indirect application to private sector businesses that:

- have or are required to have a regulatory relationship with the public sector because they conduct one or other form of licensed business activity; or
- provide goods or services to the public sector; or
- provide goods or services to other businesses that have a regulatory relationship with the public sector.

[31] Such private sector businesses will find themselves subject to commercial requirements to become and remain BEE compliant, and their compliance will be measured according to the principles and methodology of the Codes. The requirements to become and remain BEE compliant apply not only to businesses interacting with the public sector but also to those businesses interacting with the private sector suppliers and service providers to the public sector.

[32] In terms of the Codes, a business achieves BEE compliance by reference to its overall score achieved on the scorecard applicable to it, as measured by an accredited verification agency applying the verification manual, in accordance with the Codes. An entity's BEE score is measured in terms of certain 'elements' of BEE, and a certain number of maximum points can be scored for each element, namely ownership (shareholding), management control, employment equity, skills development, preferential procurement, enterprise development and socio-economic development.

[33] Entities are scored out of a possible total of 100 points. The overall performance in terms of these scorecards is then evaluated in accordance with the following scoring matrix, which indicates the BEE compliance level of entities: Level One Contributor ≥100 points; Level Two Contributor ≥85 but <100 points; Level Three Contributor ≥75 but <85 points; Level Four Contributor ≥65 but <75 points; Level Five Contributor ≥55 but <65 points; Level Six Contributor ≥45 but <55 points; Level Seven Contributor ≥40 but <45 points; Level Eight Contributor ≥30 but <40 points; Non-Compliant Contributor <30 points.

[34] Amendments to the Codes were effected in April 2015. These amendments, in essence, make it more difficult for entities to achieve the levels referred to above; i.e., the standards and thresholds have been heightened.

[35] In terms of the Codes, the only reliable evidence of the compliance of any business is a verification certificate issued annually by an accredited verification agency. Also to be borne in mind is that there are BEE 'sector charters' applicable to particular sectors of the industry. There is, for instance, a Charter for the Mining Industry and the South African Petroleum and Liquid Fuels Industry, among many others. The BEE Act and the Codes recognize sector transformation charters as evidence of the commitment by the participants in sectors that adopted them to implement BEE. Sector transformation charters are, therefore, contextual formulations of BEE. Implicit in the recognition given to sector transformation charters

in the Codes is an understanding that a formalistic application of BEE can, in certain circumstances, lead to adverse results and detract from the goals of positive social transformation that underpins South African BEE legislation. The Codes continue to be periodically amended and updated in line with developing policy considerations. During 2019, a few amendments were introduced which pertain to the so-called exempted small enterprises, qualifying small enterprises, skills development and enterprise/supplier development.

[36] The Broad-Based Black Economic Empowerment Amendment Act 46 of 2013 (Amendment Act) commenced on 24 October 2014. The following are some important amendments that were brought about by the Amendment Act into BEE law in South Africa:

- The Amendment Act introduced an offence and penalty regime, *inter alia*, for persons found guilty of BEE fronting. The implications for committing BEE fronting were, previously, only that the entity's BEE scorecard would be disqualified, and the entity would, therefore, no longer have the BEE level attributed to it by that BEE scorecard. The disqualification of an entity's scorecard and the loss of a particular BEE status did not have criminal consequences – rather having commercial consequences (e.g., the entity losing its BEE status may have warranted various contractual counterparties that it had a particular BEE status or may have been awarded a licence on the basis of having a particular BEE status and so was obliged to maintain that status or risk losing the contract or licence). Fines and imprisonment are now competent penalties for fronting and other offences.
- The Broad-Based Black Economic Empowerment Commission has been established under the Amendment Act. One of the functions of the Commission is to oversee, supervise and promote adherence with the BEE Act in the interest of the public. The Commission is also responsible for investigating any BEE initiatives either on a proactive basis or in response to a complaint.
- The Amendment Act introduces reporting obligations for South African companies. One of the functions of the Commission is to maintain a register of major BEE transactions above a threshold determined by the Minister.

5 BUSINESS FORMS/ENTERPRISES

[37] Investors have a degree of flexibility in using business forms in South Africa. Factors to be taken into account include the number of participants in the business, how the business is to be operated from a management and control point of view, achieving limited liability for participants, the requirement of perpetual succession and, importantly, income tax considerations. In the context of corporate mergers and acquisitions, one should also consider the advantages and disadvantages of using/establishing incorporated JVs as against Unincorporated Joint Ventures (UJVs), which is discussed in more detail later in the chapter. There are a number of different investment methods and vehicles available in South Africa. These are:

- a company – either a local profit or non-profit company, or a 'branch' of an external company;
- a close corporation (although new close corporations cannot be formed as of 1 May 2011);
- a partnership – either limited or unlimited;
- a business trust; and
- a sole proprietorship.

[38] A sole proprietor is where a natural person conducts business with his own assets and liabilities (without incorporating an entity). A partnership is in law not a separate legal entity but merely a contract between two or more persons with a view to conducting a profit-making venture. The partners in a partnership do not enjoy limited liability and are in fact jointly and severally liable for the partnership's debts and obligations, although this consequence can be modified with the concept of a silent partner or a so-called *en commandite* partnership. A business trust is also not a separate entity in law although the trustees of a trust do not incur personal liability, and generally speaking a third party may only look to the trust assets to satisfy its claim. However, business trusts are sometimes viewed with suspicion by the courts and can be susceptible to having their corporate veil pierced/lifted in many instances (especially if there is a commonality of trustees and beneficiaries), with the result that the trustees are held personally liable for the business debts and liabilities. Similarly, third parties may in practice be hesitant to contract with trusts. Further, the tax advantages that used to be associated with the use of trusts have been considerably eroded by tax legislation over the years, making the business trust a gradually less attractive option. Trusts feature by far more prominently in the context of estate planning of individuals, i.e., family trusts and trusts *mortis causa*.

[39] The company is by far the most popular and recommended form of legal entity in South Africa. Companies are separate legal entities. South African companies, and South African company law, in general, are modelled largely on the Commonwealth jurisdictions, although there is also a degree of influence from US corporate law. A company has shareholders (its 'owners') that contribute share capital (equity) and/or debt finance to the company and a board of directors that manages the company and its resources. The board is ultimately accountable to the shareholders. Companies may be private companies or public companies. A private company must have a restriction in its memorandum of incorporation ('MOI', which is its constitution or 'articles') on the transferability of its securities, and it is also prohibited from offering its securities to the public. It is the recommended category of company for closely held ventures with a small number of shareholders or just one shareholder. A public company, however, has no such restrictions, and its securities are therefore freely transferable, and it may offer its securities to the public. Public companies are mainly used where it is envisaged that there will be a large number of shareholders and its securities are to be traded frequently on either an over-the-counter platform or a licensed stock exchange. Public companies are, as compared to private companies, also subject to a host of additional and onerous accountability and transparency provisions under the Companies Act such as the automatic statutory requirement to have an audit committee and to have its annual financial statements audited by a registered auditor. Public companies must also have suitably qualified and experienced company secretaries.

6 THE COMPANIES ACT 71 OF 2008 AND RELATED CORPORATE LAWS

[40] The South African Companies Act came into force on 1 May 2011. Up to that point, company law in South Africa was governed for almost four decades by the Companies Act 61 of 1973, which was very much modelled on the UK company legislation at the time. The aim of the present Companies Act is to modernize company law in South Africa so that it is comparable with leading jurisdictions around the world. The Companies Act has introduced numerous new legal concepts into South African company law, and there are, therefore, some areas of uncertainty in the application and implementation of the Companies Act in these relatively early stages of its existence. Various compliance obligations have been brought about for companies and their boards, including a requirement to ensure that a company's constitutional documents are aligned with the Companies Act and that any shareholders' agreements that are in place are aligned with the company's MOI and the Companies Act. There was essentially a two-year 'grace period' for such an alignment process to take place, in that, subject to certain exceptions, for two years after the commencement date of the Companies Act, a pre-existing company's shareholders' agreement and/or constitutional documents would have prevailed in the case of any inconsistency with the Companies Act. The position currently, after the lapse of the grace period, is that a company's MOI prevails over the shareholders' agreement, and the Companies Act in turn prevails over both.

[41] The Companies Act, read with the Companies Regulations, 2011 (Regulations) promulgated thereunder, is, therefore, the key and primary piece of legislation in South Africa regulating corporate mergers and acquisitions and is supplemented in this regard by other business law statutes as well as the general principles of the law of contract (which is Roman-Dutch based, with significant influences from English law).

[42] Corporate governance and accountability are key focal areas of the Companies Act. The Companies Act requires that certain categories of companies have in place certain committees, namely audit committees (for all public and state-owned companies) and social and ethics committees (for all listed public companies and state-owned companies as well as other companies that reach a certain 'public interest score' in terms of the Regulations). The 'public interest score' takes into account the number of shareholders and employees of the company, as well as the amount of the company's third-party debt and annual turnover. The general idea behind the 'public interest score' is to subject certain large and significant private companies to the same accountability and transparency regime as is applicable to public companies.

[43] Failure to comply with the Companies Act can lead to compliance notices being issued by the Companies and Intellectual Property Commission (CIPC) (which is the regulator and registrar in respect of companies and close corporations), administrative fines and civil liability for damages caused by non-compliance. A company or director may be liable under the Companies Act to any other person for any loss or damage suffered by that person as a result of a contravention by such person of the Companies Act.

[44] The Companies Act extends shareholders' rights and recourse against companies and directors. Also, directors, prescribed officers and committee members will now face more extensive and stricter grounds for personal liability for their actions in carrying out their functions within the company than was the case under the previous regime (this is discussed in more detail later in this chapter). The Companies Act introduces class action suits against companies, directors and company officers by persons whose rights are affected by the company. Companies will thus face a greater risk of litigation and the costs thereof. Minority shareholders' rights in the context of mergers and other fundamental transactions have also been increased substantially, such as with the introduction of appraisal rights in section 164 (a remedy resembling that found in certain US states, whereby a dissenter may compel the company to purchase his/her/its shares) and the ability to set aside and review special resolutions approving such transactions under section 115. This has, however, in practice, not deterred or stifled deal activity in South Africa.

[45] The Companies Act has also introduced fairly extensive regulation of financial assistance given among related and interrelated companies, in that there must be shareholder approval, compliance with solvency and liquidity, and fairness and reasonableness in relation to such financial assistance. This, for instance, affects intra-group/inter-company loan and security arrangements, as well as transactions with third parties where guarantees or other security within a group of companies is given. This affects financial assistance given by South African companies abroad and would accordingly affect financial assistance given by South African companies to non-South African related entities. Recently published draft amendments to the Companies Act propose to limit the application of the rules pertaining to financial assistance among group companies, in that financial assistance to or for the benefit of subsidiaries will no longer be regulated.

[46] The Companies Act prohibits companies from creating any further par value shares. If a company wishes to increase its share capital, it will have to convert all of its pre-existing par value shares into shares of no par value. The revenue authorities have issued a ruling with respect to the tax treatment of such conversions to the effect that such conversions shall not be viewed as 'disposals'.

[47] An important innovation of the Companies Act is that of business rescue, contained in Chapter 6, which is modelled to some extent on the US's 'Chapter 11' bankruptcy procedures. Business rescue is a largely non-judicial, commercial process that aims to rescue a financially distressed company and maximize the likelihood of the company's continued existence on a solvent basis. There is more in-depth detail on business rescue later in this chapter.

[48] Companies in South Africa can be deregistered if they fail to timeously lodge their annual returns at the CIPC. This means that the company ceases to exist as a separate juristic person and that all of its rights and assets devolve to the state by operation of law. A company's registration can be reinstated by application to either the CIPC or the High Court. A reinstatement of a company after its deregistration is with full retrospective effect.

[49] The CIPC is responsible for registering corporate entities and intellectual property rights, maintaining information on juristic persons, ensuring compliance with and enforcing the Companies Act, and raising public awareness of company laws. It has significant functions and powers, including considering and initiating investigations of complaints and contraventions of the Companies Act and promoting voluntary dispute resolution between companies and their shareholders or directors. It is able to issue compliance notices and conclude consent orders, refer alleged offences for prosecution and refer matters to the courts or the Companies Tribunal.

[50] The Takeover Regulation Panel (Takeover Panel) is the regulator of merger activity in relation to 'Regulated Companies' (discussed in greater detail later in this chapter). The Takeover Panel often works together/concurrently with other relevant regulators such as the Johannesburg Stock Exchange (JSE).

[51] A Companies Tribunal (Tribunal) has been introduced to serve as a forum for voluntary ADR in relation to matters arising under the Companies Act and will carry out reviews of certain administrative decisions made by the Commission. The High Court remains the primary forum for dispute resolution, as well as the interpretation and enforcement of the Companies Act.

6.1 Categories of Companies

[52] The Companies Act provides for two overriding types of companies, namely 'non-profit companies' and 'profit companies'. A lighter burden is imposed on companies where all shares are owned by related parties or where all shareholders are also directors.

6.2 Non-profit Companies

[53] Non-profit companies must have at least one object, and each object must be either a 'public benefit' object (not defined in the Companies Act) or an object relating to cultural or social activities or communal or group interests. In addition, such companies may not distribute their income or property to their members and directors. They are not required to have members and can carry on any business, trade or undertaking consistent with or ancillary to their objects. Such companies do not issue shares, but instead, a person may acquire membership in such company.

[54] It is common practice in South Africa for a non-profit company to apply to be registered as a public benefit organization (PBO) with the South African Revenue

Service (SARS). If such registration is effected, the non-profit company will effectively be exempt from taxes, provided it complies with the requirements of section 30 of the Income Tax Act 58 of 1962 (Income Tax Act), read with the Ninth Schedule to the Income Tax Act. Third parties that donate to such registered PBOs benefit from tax deductions in respect of such donations.

6.3 Profit Companies

[55] These include private, personal liability, public and state-owned companies.

6.4 Private Companies

[56] The MOI of a private company must prohibit an offer of its securities to the public and must restrict the transferability of its securities. 'Securities' includes shares and debentures, as well as any other instrument issued or authorized to be issued by a profit company. It therefore includes debt instruments. The suffix attaching to a private company's name is 'Proprietary Limited' or '(Pty) Ltd'.

6.5 Personal Liability Companies

[57] The directors and past directors of such companies are jointly and severally liable together with the company for any debts and liabilities that were contracted during their respective periods of office. Personal liability companies must meet the criteria for a private company, and the MOI of such company must state that it is a personal liability company. Personal liability companies are required to be used for certain professional firms/enterprises such as law firms and auditors. The suffix attaching to a personal liability company's name is 'Incorporated' or 'Inc'.

6.6 Public Companies

[58] If a company is not a state-owned company or a personal liability company or its MOI does not satisfy both criteria for a private company (outlined above), then it is a public company. The suffix attaching to a public company's name is 'Limited' or 'Ltd'.

6.7 State-Owned Companies

[59] These are: (a) companies listed in Schedule 2 or 3 of the Public Finance Management Act 1 of 1999 (PFMA) or (b) are owned by a municipality as contemplated in the Local Government: Municipal Systems Act 32 of 2000 and are similar to an enterprise referred to in (a). They are companies owned and controlled by the state. The provisions of the Companies Act that apply to public companies also apply to state-owned companies unless the Minister has granted an exemption in respect of a category of state-owned companies. The suffix attaching to a state-owned company's name is 'SOC Ltd'. Important examples are Eskom, South African Airways and Transnet. State-owned companies are regulated by a myriad of legislation which includes the PFMA, the particular company's founding statute, administrative and procurement laws.

6.8 External Companies

[60] In terms of section 1 of the Companies Act, an external company is 'a foreign company that is carrying on business, or non-profit activities, as the case may be, within the Republic, subject to section 23(2)'. In turn, section 23(2) provides that a foreign company must be regarded as 'conducting business, or non-profit activities, as the case may be, within the Republic [of South Africa]' if that foreign company:

- is a party to one or more employment contracts within South Africa; or
- is engaging in a course of conduct, or has engaged in a course or pattern of activities within South Africa over a period of at least six months, such as would lead a person to reasonably conclude that the company intended to continually engage in business or non-profit activities within South Africa.

[61] Section 23 also sets out instances where a foreign company is not deemed to be an external company merely because it performs certain acts or transactions in South Africa, for example, acquiring immovable property here. External companies are obliged to register as such under the Companies Act by filing various documents at the CIPC. A 'branch' is established, and the external company is generally not a separate legal person, although a court may treat it as such for winding-up/insolvency purposes. It is not the case that the whole of the Companies Act applies to external companies as if they were companies incorporated under the Companies Act. A 'company' as defined in the Companies Act expressly excludes external companies, such that it is only where external companies are expressly mentioned in the Companies Act that the relevant provision will apply. There are only a handful of provisions which apply to external companies, and these are located throughout the Companies Act. An external company must:

- continuously maintain at least one office in South Africa, and register the address of its office, or its principal office if it has more than one office, with the CIPC (section 23(3));
- provide its full registered name or registration number to any person on demand, and must not misstate its name or registration number in a manner likely to mislead or deceive any person (section 32(1)); and
- file an annual return with the CIPC in the prescribed form with the prescribed fee (section 33(2)). The annual return records certain corporate and company secretarial information pertaining to the external company and is intended to assist the CIPC in keeping its registers up to date.

6.9 Accountability and Transparency

[62] Annual financial statements of companies must satisfy the prescribed financial reporting standards, which may vary for different categories of companies, and must be audited in the case of public companies. Other companies must have their financial statements audited if the Minister (after taking into account whether it is desirable in the public interest having regard to the economic or social significance of the company as indicated by a company's annual turnover, workforce size, or nature and extent of its activities) issues regulations requiring it. If not, such companies must either: (a) voluntarily elect to have their financial statements audited or (b) have them independently reviewed. Exemptions from independent review are provided for 'owner-managed' private companies where every shareholder is also a director. Impending amendments to the Companies Act will make the annual financial statements of audited private companies readily accessible to members of the public.

[63] Public companies and state-owned companies must appoint a company secretary, an auditor and an audit committee.

[64] Certain companies must also have a 'social and ethics committee'. The equivalent of the social and ethics committee in other jurisdictions is the 'corporate social responsibility' committee or 'CSR' committee. CSR is generally understood to be the recognition of the responsibility for the company's actions and the encouragement of a positive impact through its activities on the environment, consumers, employees, communities, stakeholders and all other members of the public. In terms of the Regulations, the following companies must have social and ethics committees (Regulation 43): every listed public company; every state-owned company; and any other company that has, in any two of the previous five years, scored above 500 points on its 'public interest score' in terms of Regulation 26(2). These would be significant or large private and unlisted public companies, for instance.

6.10 Corporate Finance/Capital

[65] The Companies Act contains a capital maintenance regime based on solvency and liquidity. 'Par value shares' and 'nominal value shares' are abolished. Transitional provisions provide that existing par value shares will continue in existence.

[66] Boards of companies have been given new powers to facilitate equity financing. These include the right of the board to increase or decrease the number of authorized shares of any class; to reclassify any authorized but unissued classified shares; to classify shares that are authorized but are unclassified and unissued; and to determine the preferences, rights, limitations or other terms of shares that have been authorized but not issued. The MOI may, however, exclude such powers of the board. Under the previous Companies Act 61 of 1973, alterations to share capital could only be done by special resolution of the shareholders.

[67] The Companies Act contemplates that shares can be issued for future services, future benefits or future payment. The Companies Act thus facilitates 'sweat equity', and this is a substantial relaxation on the previous rule that all issued shares had to be fully paid up. Such shares (issued for future consideration) must be issued into trust until the full subscription consideration has been paid up (section 40(5) of the Companies Act).

[68] Minority shareholders are protected by the requirement of shareholder approval for:

- issues of shares, convertible securities or share options to directors and other specified persons such as those related to the company or any director;
- substantial share issues where existing shareholders are to be diluted to the extent of 30% or more;
- financial assistance for share subscriptions or purchases; and
- loans or other financial assistance to directors or related parties.

[69] All distributions, including dividends, require board approval subject to the satisfaction of the solvency and liquidity test which is detailed in section 4 of the Companies Act. Directors who are present and participated in the decision as well as those directors who failed to vote against the distribution may be jointly and severally liable for any distribution in contravention of the Companies Act. 'Distribution' is widely defined and also includes share buy-backs, incurrences of debts or obligations for the benefit of shareholders, and waivers of debts owed by shareholders to the company. Such transactions in relation to shareholders of group companies are also covered by the definition.

[70] Provisions relating to debentures are replaced with a general scheme to protect the interests of holders of 'debt instruments' issued by a company (whether or not in the form of 'security documents') for securities other than: (a) shares or (b) promissory notes and loans and whether constituting an encumbrance on the assets of the company or not. 'Debt instruments' may be 'secured' or 'unsecured' and may have special privileges as well as allotment, redemption or substitution/conversion rights.

6.11 Company Directors, Officers and Their Duties

[71] There is no requirement that any directors or officers of a company be South African citizens or residents in South Africa, subject to what is stated below concerning the public officer and company secretary. Directors and prescribed officers must be natural persons in order to be eligible to act as such.

[72] Under the Income Tax Act, there is a requirement for a company to have a 'public officer'. A public officer is a representative taxpayer for a company, and therefore that person will serve as the face of the company for tax purposes. All actions carried out in his capacity as a public officer are deemed to have been done by the company. A company is required to appoint a public officer within one month after the company begins to carry on a business or acquires an office in

South Africa. Failure to do so will result in SARS designating a director or the company secretary as the public officer. To qualify as a public officer, a person has to be a natural person who is resident in South Africa.

[73] Private companies are not required to have company secretaries but may opt to do so. The company secretary need not be a South African citizen, and he/she may be a juristic person, but he/she must be permanently resident in South Africa while serving in that capacity.

[74] Many of the common law duties and liabilities of directors (stemming largely from English, Australian and US law) have now been codified in section 76 of the Companies Act. However, not all common law duties of directors have been codified by the Companies Act, and to this extent, they still apply concurrently with the Companies Act. Section 76 provides that a director must not use his position of director or any other information obtained while acting in his capacity as director to gain an advantage for himself/herself or any other person other than the company or a wholly owned subsidiary of the company. This obligation speaks of two important aspects of directors' duties:

(i) The 'no secret profit' and 'corporate opportunity' rules, which state that a director may not appropriate business opportunities and benefits of the company for his/her personal benefit.
(ii) The information and deliberations in the board process often encompass information which is highly confidential to the company and may harm its interests if divulged without authority. Such information may only be used for the benefit of the company or a wholly owned subsidiary.

A director may also not knowingly cause harm to the company or its subsidiary. A director must inform the board at the earliest practicable opportunity of any information of which he is aware, unless the director reasonably believes the information is immaterial to the company or generally available to the public or known to other directors, or is bound not to disclose such information by a legal or ethical obligation of confidentiality. A director of a company, when acting in that capacity, must exercise the powers and perform the functions of the director:

- in good faith and for a proper purpose. A 'proper purpose' means that the powers given to directors must be exercised for the purpose for which they were granted;
- in the best interests of the company. Linked to this duty is the common law duty to exercise an unfettered discretion; and
- with the degree of care, skill and diligence that may reasonably be expected of a person carrying out the same functions in relation to the company as those carried out by that director, and having the general knowledge, skill and experience of that director.

[75] Section 75 deals with the situation in which a director must disclose his personal financial interests, as well as those of related parties, in any matter to be considered by the company. The director must then recuse himself from the decision, and he may not vote on that matter. A director must also disclose the interests of parties 'related' to that director (this is a term defined in section 2 of the Companies Act).

[76] The 'business judgment rule' applies to South African company law. The business judgment rule provides that a director would have acted in the best interests of company and with the requisite degree of care, skill and diligence in respect of a particular matter if that director: took reasonably diligent steps to become informed about that matter; had no material personal financial interest in that matter or, if he did, followed the requisite disclosure and recusal provisions contained in section 75 of the Companies Act; and had a rational basis for believing and did believe the decision to be in best interests of company. The business judgment rule is supplemented with the 'reliance rule', in section 76(4) and (5) of the Companies Act. The reliance rule provides that, in exercising his functions as such, a director is entitled to rely on others (such as employees, committees or advisors) reporting to him, as well as opinions and information provided to him. In basic terms, reliance is well founded if the director reasonably believes that the persons advising or reporting to him merit confidence.

[77] For purposes of the sections of the Companies Act dealing with directors' eligibility, disqualifications, duties, responsibilities and personal liability, a 'director' is defined to include:

- a prescribed officer; and
- a person who is a member of a committee of a board of a company, or an audit committee, irrespective of whether the person is also a member of the company's board.

This means that, for purposes of the sections in question, prescribed officers and members of committees are treated in the same way as directors, irrespective of whether or not these persons are members of the board of directors. A 'prescribed officer' is defined as a person who exercises general executive control over and management of the whole, or a significant portion, of the business and activities of the company, or regularly participates to a material degree in the exercise of general executive control over and management of the whole, or a significant portion, of the business and activities of the company.

6.12 Fundamental Transactions, Mergers: General Points and Framework

[78] Merger and acquisition law in South Africa is modern and fluid. Broadly, an acquisition can take place in respect of either the shares of a company or its business/assets. In the context of private companies, a simple sale of shares or subscription for shares agreement can be concluded (this is often regulated simply by the general principles of the law of contract), or the 'fundamental transaction' mechanisms in the Companies Act may be utilized.

[79] The 'fundamental transactions' governed by Part A of Chapter 5 of the Companies Act encompass:

- the disposal of all or the greater part of the assets or undertaking of a company;
- schemes of arrangement; and
- amalgamations and mergers.

These are discussed in turn under 'The Specific Fundamental Transactions' below. Under the Companies Act, fundamental transactions require shareholder approval by way of a special resolution of the company that is subject to the transaction. Such resolution may, in certain circumstances, have to be reviewed and confirmed by the High Court if there are objections to the resolution by dissenting shareholders. Where a fundamental transaction or other takeover is implemented in respect of any company, a number of requirements must be met and approvals obtained, other than those of the Companies Act and Takeover Law which are discussed in greater detail later in this chapter. Examples follow.

[80] To the extent that the transaction involves the offering of securities in one company to the shareholders of another company, consideration should be given to whether such offer amounts to an 'offer to the public' as contemplated in Chapter 4 of the Companies Act. If so, this may necessitate the preparation of a prospectus which must be registered at the CIPC. This could be particularly relevant if the target company is a listed company with thousands of shareholders, which would almost certainly comprise a 'section of the public' as contemplated in Chapter 4.

[81] If the parties to the transaction are listed on the stock exchange operated by the JSE Limited, certain JSE Listings Requirements (Listing Requirements) may be applicable. Very often, shareholder approval would be required under the Listings Requirements, and the Listings Requirements also contain timetables for the implementation of corporate actions and fundamental transactions which have to be adhered to. The Listings Requirements classify transactions into Category '1' or '2', depending on the so-called percentage ratio of the transaction. The percentage ratio is determined with reference to the consideration of market capitalization ratio, the dilution factor or, in the case of settlement partly in cash and partly by the issue of shares in the acquiring company, a combination of the two. The following are the requirements for Categories 1 and 2 transactions:

- Category 2 transactions: a Category 2 transaction is a transaction where any percentage ratio is 5% or more, but each ratio is less than 30%. In the case of a Category 2 transaction, the company must publish an announcement. Shareholder approval is not required.
- Category 1 transactions: a Category 1 transaction is a transaction where any percentage ratio is 30% or more or if the total consideration is not subject to any maximum. Upon the terms of a Category 1 transaction being agreed, the company must: (i) comply with the Category 2 requirements and state within the announcement that the transaction is subject to shareholders' approval and that a circular to shareholders will be issued, and (ii) within sixty days, the company will need to dispatch a circular to shareholders containing a notice of general meeting to obtain their approval.

The 'percentage ratios' referred to above are as follows:

- Consideration of market capitalization: is the consideration that is payable or receivable divided by the total market value of all the listed equity securities, excluding treasury securities, of the listed company.
- Dilution: is the number of listed equity securities that will be issued by a listed company as consideration for an acquisition, compared to those in issue, excluding treasury securities, prior to the transaction.
- Transactions to be settled partly in cash and partly in shares: one should first assess the cash-to-market capitalization percentage and then add this calculated percentage to the dilution percentage.

The Listings Requirements also regulate 'related party' transactions. Special requirements apply to transactions between a listed company and related parties. 'Related parties' are defined as including a material shareholder, a director, an adviser, a principal executive of the company, or any person who occupied any of these positions within twelve months immediately preceding the date of the transaction. Due to the special nature of related party transactions, a listed company is required to undertake additional obligations in respect of those transactions. These additional obligations entail requiring an announcement to be made equivalent to that required for a Category 2 transaction, furnishing the proposed agreement to the JSE, sending a circular to the company's shareholders, and obtaining the approval of the listed company's shareholders, including a resolution passed by the shareholders other than the related party and its associates. Furthermore, the listed company is required to obtain an opinion from an independent professional expert that the terms of the proposed transaction are fair as far as the shareholders of the listed company are concerned.

[82] Depending on the size of the transaction and the parties thereto, merger control provisions in South African law may apply. Under the Competition Act 89 of 1998, the approval of the Competition Commission or the Competition Tribunal may be required before a change of control is implemented. In order for merger control to be relevant, the threshold is that the combination of the annual turnover in, into or from South Africa or the gross asset values in South Africa of the acquiring group and the transferred firm (target) equal or exceed ZAR600 m, and either the annual turnover in, into or from South Africa or the gross asset values in South Africa of the transferred firm equal or exceed ZAR100 m. Merger control is discussed in more detail under the relevant sections dealing with competition law.

[83] If any of the parties to the transaction are entities which are regulated within a particular sector of the economy, sometimes the consent of the sector regulator (if any) is required for the transaction to be implemented, as the regulatory legislation in question often prescribes that a change of control requires approval. Examples are entities that operate under a licence such as banks, mining companies, insurance companies, telecommunications and those that operate gambling activities – changes of control in respect of these types of companies invariably require the approval of the applicable regulator.

[84] Exchange control approval would be relevant if non-South African resident entities are involved in the transaction, particularly where cash or securities are to be transferred, or financial assistance is to be provided, across the border.

[85] One should at all times be mindful of insider trading laws as well as the provisions relating to the disclosure of inside information if one is dealing with listed securities. South African inside information rules are principally contained in the Financial Markets Act (FMA) 19 of 2012 and, to some extent, in the Listings Requirements.

[86] Approvals and consents under private agreements may need to be sought – for example, waivers of pre-emptive rights in respect of securities or immovable property.

6.13 The Specific Fundamental Transactions

[87] In terms of section 112 of the Companies Act, a company may not dispose of all or the greater part of its assets or undertaking (i.e., over 50% of the gross assets/undertaking) unless it has complied with the various requirements of sections 112 and 115. This would typically occur upon the sale of a major business or asset. The special measures include a special resolution of shareholders, taken in the normal manner, but subject to complying with the additional requirements of section 115. Although the issue is debatable, the predominant view among practitioners in the market appears to be that the approval under section 115 must be procured at a meeting and cannot be done by way of a written resolution (round-robin). An argument in this regard is that the application of the appraisal rights in section 164 may be unworkable in the context of round-robins, having regard to the numerous procedures and steps that have to be taken under section 164 in order for a dissenting shareholder to exercise his/her/its rights. Any part of the undertaking or assets to be disposed of must be fairly valued, as calculated in the prescribed manner, as at the date of the proposal which date must also be determined in the prescribed manner.

[88] The scheme of arrangement contemplated in section 114 of the Companies Act remains an effective and popular method for takeovers and reconstructions, especially in the listed environment. This remains the case despite the introduction of the new statutory merger mechanism under section 113, read with section 116 (which is discussed below). Greater clarity and simplicity have been introduced by providing for a specific procedure for solvent companies. Significantly, schemes of arrangement are no longer a court-sanctioned process (as compared to the position in, for instance, the UK or Australia). Unless it is in liquidation or in the course of business rescue proceedings, the board of a company may propose any arrangement between the company and the holders of any class of its securities by way of any of a range of methods, namely:

- a consolidation of securities of different classes;
- a division of securities into different classes;

- an expropriation of securities from the holders;
- exchanging any of its securities for other securities;
- a reacquisition by the company of its securities; or
- a combination of the methods contemplated above.

The company must retain an independent expert who must compile a report to the board regarding the proposed arrangement that must also be distributed to the holders of the company's securities. The expert must meet certain requirements relating to qualification, competence, experience and independence. The report must cover certain minimum particulars about the arrangement, including the material effects that the proposed arrangement will have on the rights and interests of the holders of the relevant class of securities and an evaluation of any material adverse effects compared to the compensation or probable beneficial effects for the relevant persons. As is the case of the other fundamental transactions, a scheme of arrangement must, in terms of section 115 of the Companies Act, be approved by a special resolution of those entitled to exercise voting rights on the matter, and the minority holders of such voting rights have various rights, including appraisal rights, at their disposal. South Africa has an extensive and highly developed jurisprudence on compromises and schemes of arrangement.

[89] Regarding the statutory merger and amalgamation contemplated in section 113 of the Companies Act, the following few key features of this new procedure in South African company law, which has been adopted primarily from the US and Canadian law, may be mentioned:

- A profit company may amalgamate or merge with another profit company by using the mechanisms in section 113 and ensuring that there is a written merger agreement which sets out how the transaction is structured and implemented. Only South African companies may merge/amalgamate with each other.
- In drafts of the Companies Bill, a distinction was drawn between an 'amalgamation' whereby a company undergoes a 'fusion' of equals with another company and a new amalgamated entity is formed, and a 'merger' whereby one company subsumes the other. However, the drafters ultimately settled on providing for the same regime and principles in respect of both mergers and amalgamations.
- The defining feature of the amalgamation or merger is that, once it is implemented, the assets and liabilities of the amalgamating or merging companies vest, by operation of law, in the amalgamated or merged company or companies as set out in a merger agreement.

The board of each amalgamating or merging company must consider whether each amalgamated or merged company will satisfy the solvency and liquidity test set out in section 4(1) of the Companies Act. If the board reasonably believes this will be the case, the merger agreement can be submitted to the shareholders of the amalgamating or merging company for approval by special resolution, in terms of section 115 of the Act. In a similar fashion to the other two fundamental transactions, the notice convening the meeting must contain the merger agreement and explain the rights of minorities in terms of section 115 and the appraisal rights governed by section 164 of the Companies Act. The new statutory merger mechanism has yet to feature prominently on the South African corporate acquisitions scene; however, it is a very useful mechanism for intra-group restructurings.

6.14 The Takeover Laws

[90] In South Africa, the laws relating to mergers and takeovers (Takeover Law) are not codified in a single instrument. A number of pieces of legislation and other sources have to be taken into consideration. The principal sources of Takeover Law are as follows:

- Parts B and C of Chapter 5 of the Companies Act (sections 117–127).
- The Takeover Regulations, which supplement and elaborate on the Companies Act's provisions.
- High Court cases dealing with Takeover Laws.
- The guidelines and rulings of the Takeover Panel which are published from time to time on the Takeover Panel's website.
- The previous regime pertaining to takeovers in South Africa, as contained in the Companies Act 61 of 1973 and the Securities Regulation Panel Code on Takeovers and Mergers, as well as the case law thereunder, is still relevant and useful to the extent that the old and new regimes correspond.
- The Companies Act expressly permits our courts and tribunals to consider foreign law to the extent appropriate. It is not unusual for the Takeover Panel, for instance, to consider the UK or Hong Kong takeover codes and the notes/commentary therein if their provisions are similar to South African Takeover Laws.

[91] Before the Takeover Laws apply, first, it needs to be established whether the transaction involves a company, as target/offeree, which is regulated in terms of the Takeover Laws (Regulated Company). The South African Takeover Laws regulate only South African incorporated companies that are the subject of one of the listed categories of transactions involving a takeover or change of control of a Regulated Company (Affected Transaction). It is irrelevant whether the other transaction parties (e.g., the acquirer) are South African companies or even Regulated Companies – the question is whether the subject of the Affected Transaction or the 'target' (and in some instances, its subsidiaries) is a Regulated Company.

[92] In order to be a Regulated Company, the company must be either of the following:

- a public company;
- a state-owned company;
- a private company which is a Regulated Company if more than 10% of its voting securities were transferred in the previous twenty-four months among persons that are not related or interrelated. However, even if a private company does not fall within the statutory criterion of a Regulated Company, a private company may, in terms of its MOI, voluntarily submit itself to the Takeover Laws, although this is rarely seen in practice as the company and its

shareholders would typically not want to be subject to an additional layer of regulation should a potential takeover be proposed in respect of the company. Impending amendments to the Companies Act will introduce an entirely new test in respect of private companies which will depend on the number of direct and indirect shareholders of a company (ten or more) and the company's assets or turnover value.

[93] Once it is established that one is concerned with a Regulated Company, the next question is whether an 'Affected Transaction' is proposed to be implemented in respect of the Regulated Company. The Affected Transactions are listed in section 117(1)(c) of the Companies Act and are as follows (the first three are the 'fundamental transactions' that were described earlier):

- Major disposal. The first Affected Transaction is a disposal of all or the greater part of the assets or undertaking of a Regulated Company, as contemplated in section 112. That section essentially concerns sales of business, but there need not necessarily be a sale of a going concern in order to trigger that provision. Section 112 provides that where a company proposes to dispose of more than 50% of its assets or undertaking, fairly valued, it requires shareholder approval by way of a special resolution (i.e., at least 75% of the voting rights exercised on the resolution).
- Merger or amalgamation. An amalgamation or merger, as contemplated in section 113, is an Affected Transaction if it involves at least one Regulated Company. A profit company may amalgamate or merge with another profit company by using the mechanisms in section 113 and ensuring that there is a written merger agreement which sets out how the transaction is structured and implemented.
- Scheme of arrangement. A scheme of arrangement is a mechanism found in the company law of many jurisdictions across the globe. In many jurisdictions, it is a court-sanctioned process, as was the case in South Africa until the commencement of the Companies Act. Under the Companies Act, however, the requirement of the court's sanction has been replaced by the requirement that an independent expert's report on the fairness and reasonableness of the scheme be distributed to the company's security holders.
- Multiples of 5% share acquisitions. An Affected Transaction occurs where a person acquires a beneficial interest in sufficient securities of a class issued by a Regulated Company such that, as a result of the acquisition, the person holds a beneficial interest in voting securities amounting to 5%, 10%, 15%, or any further whole multiple of 5%, of the issued securities of that class. The Takeover Panel has issued a guideline which provides that for this category of Affected Transaction the prior clearance or approval of the Takeover Panel is not required. There is nevertheless a disclosure/reporting requirement for such acquisitions in section 122 of the Companies Act: disclosures need to be made to the issuer of the securities, to the issuer's security holders, and to the Takeover Panel.
- Acquisition of remaining voting securities. An Affected Transaction occurs where there is an announced intention to acquire a beneficial interest in the remaining voting securities of a Regulated Company not already held by a

person, or persons acting in concert. Thus, for example, if a shareholder presently holds 20% of the shares and launches an offer to acquire the remaining voting securities not held by that shareholder, that offer would be regulated by the Takeover Laws.

- Mandatory offers. A mandatory offer to remaining holders of voting securities as contemplated in section 123 of the Companies Act, which is required to be made where a person crosses the 'bright line' of 35% shareholding in a Regulated Company, is an Affected Transaction. There are regulations dealing with the determination of the price at which this mandatory offer must be made. In basic terms, it must be the highest price paid by the acquirer or its concert parties for the acquisition of voting securities of that class within the previous six months. Comparable offers must be made to holders of different classes of voting securities.
- Compulsory acquisitions. Section 124 of the Companies Act deals with instances in which an offeror can 'squeeze out' the minority shareholders of a Regulated Company (i.e., compulsorily acquire their voting securities), as well as the converse, namely where the minority can compel an offeror to buy them out. It is important to note that these compulsory acquisition provisions apply only where there was an offer in the first place and which was accepted by a certain number of offerees. The threshold is 90%. The rationale behind section 124 is that a supermajority and a superminority have been created as a result of the level of acceptances in respect of the offer, the supermajority should be given the right to squeeze out the superminority, and, conversely, the latter should be given the right to compel the former to squeeze them out. The process of the squeeze-out is an Affected Transaction.

[94] A number of factors are taken into consideration in determining which method, or which Affected Transaction, is to be utilized in effecting a takeover of a Regulated Company. One of the key considerations at the outset is whether the transaction is 'friendly' (i.e., the board of directors of the target company is amenable to the takeover and is prepared to facilitate it) or the opposite (a 'hostile' takeover). The first three Affected Transactions listed above (major disposal, merger or amalgamation, scheme of arrangement) are only possible if the basis is 'friendly' because these methods require the board of the target to propose the transaction to its shareholders for their approval by way of a special resolution. If the takeover is 'hostile', the acquirer would have to launch an offer directly to the target's shareholders by way of a general offer (commonly also referred to as a 'tender offer'). Apart from this, considerations relating to the acquisition of shares versus assets (including the assumption of the target company's liabilities), squeeze-out thresholds and tax implications will all play a role.

[95] Section 48 of the Companies Act, which deals with the acquisition by a company of its own shares, provides that if a company buys back more than 5% of a class of its shares, that acquisition 'is subject to the requirements of sections 114 and 115'. Section 114 deals with schemes of arrangement. An interpretation that has some support in practice is that such a buy-back is in fact a scheme of arrangement, and it then follows that if it is implemented in respect of a Regulated Company, one is concerned with an Affected Transaction, and therefore the Takeover Laws apply.

However, the most recent amendments to the Companies Act will clarify that such buy-backs are not schemes of arrangement and are subject only to a special resolution of shareholders unless pursuant to a pro rata offer to all shareholders or are executed on a stock exchange.

[96] The main significances of the Takeover Laws (some of which are discussed in more detail below) are as follows:

- The Takeover Panel regulates the transaction.
- All documents posted or published in connection with the transaction must be approved in advance by the Takeover Panel. This entails additional costs as the Takeover Panel charges fees based on the value of the transaction. The Takeover Panel's turnaround times are, however, fortunately speedy and efficient, and, therefore, one typically does not run into difficulties from a timing perspective in this regard, as long as one's documents are compliant with the Takeover Regulations.
- There are restrictions on the board of the offeree Regulated Company/target from taking steps and actions that would frustrate the offer.
- There are restrictions on, and regulation of, dealings by the offeror in securities of the target before and during an offer. This is to ensure a degree of stability and to ensure that favourable terms are not being extended to some of the target's shareholders that are not being extended to others.
- The offeree Regulated Company must establish an independent board to consider and opine on the offer.
- The independent board may be required by the Takeover Panel to appoint an independent expert with respect to the offer consideration.
- The Takeover Law prescribes a number of processes and timing requirements which must be adhered to in the course of an Affected Transaction.
- The Takeover Regulations prescribe a host of information and details which must be contained in the circular that is sent to the target's shareholders.

[97] In South Africa, the regulator in respect of Takeover Law is the Takeover Panel, an institution which is comparable in its role and functions to, for instance, the Panel on Takeovers and Mergers in the UK and the Securities Commissions in the US and Canada.

[98] The law requires that the Takeover Panel must regulate any Affected Transaction or offer, but without regard to the commercial advantages or disadvantages of any transaction or proposed transaction, in order to ensure the integrity of the marketplace and fairness to the holders of the securities of Regulated Companies, to ensure the provision of necessary information to holders of securities of Regulated Companies to the extent required to facilitate the making of fair and informed decisions and of adequate time to obtain and provide advice with respect to offers, and to prevent actions by a Regulated Company designed to impede, frustrate, or defeat an offer or the making of fair and informed decisions by the holders of that company's securities. Further, the Takeover Panel must regulate the Affected Transaction in a manner that ensures that no person may enter into an Affected Transaction unless that person is ready, able and willing to implement that transaction; that all holders of any particular class of securities of an offeree Regulated Company are afforded equivalent treatment; that no relevant information is withheld from the holders of relevant securities; and that all holders of relevant securities receive the same information in an Affected Transaction.

[99] The Takeover Panel may also exempt an Affected Transaction from compliance with the Takeover Laws if there is no reasonable potential of the Affected Transaction prejudicing the interests of any existing holder of a Regulated Company's securities, the cost of compliance is disproportionate, relative to the value of the Affected Transaction, or doing so is otherwise reasonable and justifiable in the circumstances having regard to the principles and purposes of Takeover Law. The exemption route is typically used only where one is dealing with a private company, where all the shareholders are prepared to execute waivers, and where the usual requirements such as constituting an independent board and preparing circulars are simply too onerous when compared to the size and nature of the companies and the transaction. It would not be possible where, for instance, the target is a public listed company, in which case one has to comply with all the Takeover Laws and obtain a clearance certificate from the Takeover Panel.

6.15 Business Rescue and Compromises

[100] The Companies Act contains a 'business rescue' regime aimed at facilitating the rehabilitation of companies that are 'financially distressed'. The business rescue procedure takes cognizance of the success of Chapter 11 bankruptcy provisions in the US and of corporate rescue provisions in other overseas jurisdictions. The Companies Act also provides separately, in section 155, for a court-sanctioned compromise process whereby claims of creditors may be compromised and rearranged.

[101] The Companies Act contains provisions in terms of which an 'affected person' (shareholders, creditors, employees, trade unions) may cause the affairs of the company to be placed under the control of a turnaround expert or business rescue practitioner. 'Business rescue' means proceedings to facilitate the rehabilitation of a company that is financially distressed by providing for: (i) the temporary supervision of the company and of the management of its affairs, business and property; (ii) a temporary moratorium on the rights of claimants against the company or in respect of property in its possession; and (iii) the development and implementation, if approved, of a plan to rescue the company by restructuring its affairs, business, property, debt and other liabilities, and equity in a manner that maximizes the likelihood of the company continuing in existence on a solvent basis or, if it is not possible for the company to so continue in existence, results in a better return for the company's creditors or shareholders than would result from the immediate liquidation of the company.

[102] These provisions primarily apply when a company is 'financially distressed', which in terms of the Companies Act means that it appears to be:

- reasonably unlikely that the company will be able to pay all of its debts as they become due and payable within the immediately ensuing six months; or
- reasonably likely that the company will become insolvent within the immediately ensuing six months.

[103] During business rescue proceedings, there is a general moratorium on legal proceedings against the company. The practitioner has full management control of the company in substitution for its board. He must investigate the company's affairs, business, property and financial situation. There are also provisions in the Companies Act enabling the practitioner to raise finance for the operations of the company, and he can secure such finance over assets of the company which are not otherwise encumbered.

[104] The business rescue plan, which in terms of the overarching 'cram-down' principle becomes binding on all creditors and shareholders once adopted by the requisite majorities of those stakeholders, must contain all the information reasonably required to facilitate affected persons in deciding whether or not to accept or reject the plan, and must be divided into three parts, as follows:

- Part A – Background, which must include at least: a complete list of all the material assets of the company, as well as an indication as to which assets were held as security by creditors when the business rescue proceedings began; a complete list of the creditors of the company when the business rescue proceedings began, as well as an indication as to which creditors would qualify as secured, statutory preferent and concurrent in terms of the laws of insolvency, and an indication of which of the creditors have proved their claims; the probable dividend that would be received by creditors, in their specific classes, if the company were to be placed in liquidation; a complete list of the holders of the company's issued securities; a copy of the written agreement concerning the practitioner's remuneration; and a statement whether the business rescue plan includes a proposal made informally by a creditor of the company.
- Part B – Proposals, which must include at least: the nature and duration of any moratorium for which the business rescue plan makes provision; the extent to which the company is to be released from the payment of its debts, and the extent to which any debt is proposed to be converted to equity in the company, or another company; the ongoing role of the company, and the treatment of any existing agreements; the property of the company that is to be available to pay creditors' claims in terms of the business rescue plan; the order of preference in which the proceeds of property will be applied to pay creditors if the business rescue plan is adopted; the benefits of adopting the business rescue plan as opposed to the benefits that would be received by creditors if the company were to be placed in liquidation; and the effect that the business rescue plan will have on the holders of each class of the company's issued securities.
- Part C – Assumptions and conditions, which must include at least: a statement of the conditions that must be satisfied, if any, for the business rescue plan to come into operation and be fully implemented; the effect, if any, that

the business rescue plan contemplates on the number of employees, and their terms and conditions of employment; the circumstances in which the business rescue plan will end; and a projected balance sheet for the company and statement of income and expenses for the ensuing three years.

6.16 Financial Assistance

[105] Similar to what is found in a number of Commonwealth jurisdictions, South African company law regulates and restricts the provision of financial assistance in connection with the acquisition of a company's shares. For many years, in South African law, such financial assistance was prohibited due to the capital maintenance rules, but since 2006, the corporate laws have been amended to relax the prohibition, subject to a number of requirements and safeguards. Currently, section 44 of the Companies Act deals with financial assistance given in connection with the acquisition of 'securities' of a company or of a related company. 'Securities' includes shares but is a wider concept and includes other instruments issued by a profit company such as debentures, notes, bonds, etc. Except to the extent that the MOI of a company provides otherwise, the board may authorize the company to provide financial assistance by way of a loan, guarantee, the provision of security or otherwise to any person for the purpose of, or in connection with, the subscription of any option, or any securities, issued or to be issued by the company or a related or interrelated company, or for the purchase of any securities of the company or a related or interrelated company, subject to the conditions and requirements described below.

[106] 'Financial assistance' does not include the lending of money in the ordinary course of business by a company whose primary business is the lending of money.

[107] The board may not authorize any financial assistance contemplated above unless:

(1) the particular provision of financial assistance is:
   (a) pursuant to an employee share scheme that satisfies the requirements of section 97; or
   (b) pursuant to a special resolution of the shareholders, adopted within the previous two years, which approved such assistance either for the specific recipient or generally for a category of potential recipients, and the specific recipient falls within that category.

(2) the board is satisfied that:
   (a) immediately after providing the financial assistance, the company would satisfy the solvency and liquidity test; and
   (b) the terms under which the financial assistance is proposed to be given are fair and reasonable to the company.

[108] There is no exhaustive definition of 'financial assistance' in the Companies Act for purposes of section 44. Instead, the Act refers only to examples, but these do not comprise an exhaustive list. The specific examples are the lending of money; guaranteeing a loan or other obligation; and securing any debt or obligation. Other examples which would typically be captured by section 44 are suretyships; any security, such as bonds and security cessions and pledges; 'letters of comfort', depending on the wording and purposes thereof; indemnities; certain share subscriptions (e.g., where a company chooses to capitalize another company by means of an 'equity injection' instead of a shareholder loan), depending on the purpose of such share subscription; and subordination agreements where, for example, a company subordinates its claim against a party for the benefit of a third-party financier.

[109] The solvency and liquidity test is contained in section 4 of the Companies Act. The test requires two types of 'solvency', i.e., factual as well as commercial solvency. Factual solvency is purely a balance sheet test; i.e., at a particular moment, it must appear, based on all reasonably foreseeable financial circumstances, that assets are in excess of liabilities. In respect of liquidity, it must appear, based on all reasonably foreseeable financial circumstances, that the company will be able to pay its debts as they fall due in the ordinary course of business for twelve months after the test was applied. The purpose of the fairness and reasonableness requirement in section 44 is to avoid the prejudice which may be suffered by the company's third-party creditors and shareholders if the company were to advance loans on 'soft' terms, thereby diminishing the company's assets/resources. The following factors may presumably be taken into account in assessing the 'fairness and reasonableness' of the financial assistance:

- whether, in view of the financial position of the parties, the loan should have been made or the security should have been provided at all;
- in the case of a loan, whether security has been or should in the circumstances have been provided therefor, and whether any security provided therefor is adequate;
- the consideration for the loan or security, including any interest or other benefit received therefor;
- the term of the loan or security; and
- the manner of repayment of the loan or discharge of the security.

[110] Another important financial assistance provision in the Companies Act is section 45. It regulates the provision of financial assistance to company directors, prescribed officers and group companies. Its provisions and requirements largely mirror those of section 44 discussed above.

6.17 Statutory Minority Protections

[111] The Companies Act contains extensive protections of shareholders' rights. Section 163 of the Companies Act provides a remedy for shareholders in the case of oppressive or unfairly prejudicial conduct. A court can come to the assistance of a member if the member satisfies the court that an act or omission of the company or a related person or the manner in which it has conducted its affairs is unfairly prejudicial, unjust or inequitable, or unfairly disregards the interests of the applicant. The court has wide powers to provide an appropriate remedy, which includes appointing a liquidator (if the company appears to be insolvent) or placing the company under supervision in terms of the business rescue provisions of the Companies Act. However, in reaching its decision, a court would take account of the underlying motives of the majority in deciding whether particular conduct requires relief. The courts uphold the general principle that by becoming a shareholder a person undertakes to be bound by the decisions of the prescribed majority of shareholders, provided that these are in accordance with the law. Accordingly, mere dissatisfaction with the conduct of the company's affairs will not of itself constitute grounds of prejudice, injustice or inequity within the meaning of the section.

[112] In terms of section 20(4), one or more shareholders may apply to the High Court for an appropriate order to restrain the company from doing anything inconsistent with the Companies Act. If the powers or capacity of the company are limited, restricted or qualified in any way in its MOI, in terms of section 20(5), one or more shareholders may apply to the High Court for an appropriate order to restrain the company or the directors from doing anything inconsistent with any such limitation, restriction or qualification. In terms of section 20(6), each shareholder of a company has a claim for damages against any person who intentionally, fraudulently or due to gross negligence causes the company to do anything inconsistent with the Companies Act or a limitation, restriction or qualification on its powers or capacity as contemplated above, unless that action has been ratified by the shareholders by way of a special resolution.

[113] Section 71(3) contains a mechanism whereby any shareholder (or director) can set in motion a process to remove a director who the shareholder feels is unfit to hold that office. This process is triggered if the shareholder alleges that a director is ineligible or disqualified from being a director, or is incapacitated to the extent that the director is unable to perform the functions of a director, and is unlikely to regain that capacity within a reasonable time, or has neglected, or been derelict in the performance of, the functions of a director. Once such an allegation is made, the board of the company must call a meeting to determine whether to remove the director in question. If the board decides not to remove the director, the aggrieved shareholder can apply to the court to review the decision of the board. In instances where the board consists of two or fewer directors, the shareholder must apply directly to the Companies Tribunal to remove the director on the grounds referred to above.

[114] Further, there is a mechanism contained in section 162 of the Companies Act in terms of which any shareholder (although this remedy also extends to, *inter alia*, directors of a company) may apply to a court to declare a particular director of the company to be 'delinquent', thereby disqualifying him from acting as a director of any company. The grounds for delinquency mainly relate to gross abuse of a director's position, gross negligence and breach of trust, among other grounds.

[115] There is also a mechanism whereby shareholder resolutions in respect of mergers and acquisitions may be reviewed by a court. Even if a company has successfully passed a special resolution approving a fundamental transaction or a share buy-back envisaged in section 48(8) (i.e., it has obtained the requisite majority of 75% or such other percentage specified in its MOI), minority shareholders (regardless of the size of their shareholding) still have recourse to court to set aside the special resolution, in terms of section 115(3).

[116] A court may only set aside the special resolution if:

- the resolution is manifestly unfair to any class of holders of the company's securities; or
- the vote was materially tainted by conflict of interest, inadequate disclosure, failure to comply with the Companies Act, the MOI of the company or any applicable rules of the company, or other significant and material procedural irregularity.

[117] Appraisal rights constitute a critical minority protection. Where a company proposes to conclude a fundamental transaction or to amend its MOI in a manner which materially adversely affects the rights of a class of shareholders (Appraisal Right Triggers), dissenting minority shareholders can, in terms of section 164, compel the company to purchase that shareholder's shares at fair value. This is the so-called appraisal right. There are numerous steps that need to be taken by a dissenting shareholder in exercising this right, both before and after the shareholders' meeting takes place. The basic premise of the appraisal remedy is that any shareholder is entitled to 'exit' the company at fair value if the company obtains all the requisite approvals and goes ahead in implementing transactions that amount to Appraisal Right Triggers.

[118] Lastly, in many instances throughout the Companies Act, shareholder approval by special resolution is required for certain transactions to be effected by a company which could potentially have an adverse effect on shareholders' interests. In order to be passed, special resolutions require a minimum of 75% of the shareholder votes exercised to be cast in favour of the resolution (but a company may, in its MOI, increase or decrease this percentage). Therefore, a shareholder holding over 25% of the shares could block every such resolution. The important instances in which special resolutions are required are to:

- amend the company's MOI;
- ratify actions by the company or directors in excess of their authority due to a company's restricted capacity;
- approve an issue of shares or grant of rights in the circumstances contemplated in section 41. These relate to fresh issues of shares: (i) to directors, prescribed officers or persons related or interrelated to them; (ii) to persons related or interrelated to the company or (iii) where the issue of shares will dilute the voting rights in a class by 30% or more;
- authorize the board to grant financial assistance in the circumstances contemplated in section 44 (dealing with financial assistance in connection with the acquisition of securities of the company or of related or interrelated companies) or section 45 (dealing with financial assistance in general to, *inter alia*, directors and prescribed officers of the company and to related or interrelated companies or corporations of the company);

- approve a decision of the board for the reacquisition of shares (i.e., a share buy-back) in the circumstances contemplated in section 48(8), which refers to reacquisitions from directors or prescribed officers or persons related to them, or where more than 5% of a class of shares is to be reacquired;
- authorize the basis for compensation to directors of a profit company (director fees);
- approve the voluntary winding-up of the company; and
- approve any proposed fundamental transaction (discussed earlier in this chapter).

6.18 Insider Trading

[119] The provisions governing insider trading in South Africa are based on legislation in the UK and the US. In essence, a person is prohibited from trading in the securities of a listed company after obtaining information about its affairs and before such information becomes publicly known, where such information, if publicly known, would materially affect the value of such securities. A person contravening this prohibition commits a criminal offence and will be liable in a civil action to someone who has suffered loss or damage as a result of the contravention. There are also prohibitions on the disclosure of inside information which must be closely considered in the context of due diligence investigations on listed target companies. In February 2020, the National Treasury announced a proposed substantial review and overhaul of the laws governing regulated securities markets, and, thus, the South African legal landscape in this regard is anticipated to undergo important changes.

[120] Insider trading is currently regulated by the FMA 19 of 2012. The FMA encompasses all financial instruments and securities regardless of whether such financial instruments or securities are issued by a South African company and regardless of whether the transaction takes place on a stock exchange or over-the-counter. Any person convicted is liable to a substantial fine or imprisonment of up to ten years, or both. It is not necessary to prove that the knowledge of the inside information influenced, or was the cause of, the trade.

[121] Under the FMA, the Directorate of Market Abuse (the Directorate) is given powers to investigate insider trading and to institute civil proceedings in relation thereto. The proceeds of civil proceedings must be deposited in a trust account, and the Directorate administers the proof of claims by third parties adversely affected by the insider trading and distribution of payments to such claimants. An individual is not precluded from pursuing any common law rights he or she may have against an insider trader, but any amount received from the Directorate will be taken into account when calculating the quantum of any claim.

[122] The FMA also gives the Directorate wide investigative powers, including rights of attachment, removal of documents, interrogation and interdict (injunction).

6.19 Share Repurchases

[123] Pursuant to section 48 of the Companies Act, a company may acquire its own shares. A redemption of shares in accordance with the terms and conditions of such share is not subject to section 48. A share buy-back is treated as a distribution to shareholders. No share buy-back is permitted unless the board reasonably believes that the company would, after the payment, be able to pay its own debts as they become due in the ordinary course of business, and if the assets of the company fairly valued would after the payment be more than the consolidated liabilities of the company (the solvency and liquidity test). Shares acquired are cancelled as issued shares but remain as part of the authorized share capital. For listed companies, there is fairly extensive regulation of share buy-backs under the Listings Requirements.

[124] Subsidiary companies are permitted, under section 48, to acquire up to 10% of the total number of issued shares of their holding company. However, the subsidiaries may not vote for such shares. This is South African law's version of 'treasury shares'.

[125] A decision by the board of the company to conclude a share buy-back in terms of section 48 of the Companies Act:

- must be approved by special resolution of the shareholders if any shares are to be acquired by the company from a director or prescribed officer of the company or any person related to a director or prescribed officer of the company; and
- is subject to the Companies Act's requirements in relation to schemes of arrangement (section 114) and fundamental transactions (section 115) if the share buy-back considered alone or together with other transactions in an integrated series of transactions involves the company acquiring more than 5% of the issued shares of any particular class of its shares.

Impending amendments to the Companies Act will simplify the regime on share buy-backs and will provide that all buy-backs are subject only to a special resolution of shareholders unless executed pursuant to a general pro rata offer or on a stock exchange.

6.20 Payments to Shareholders

[126] A company may, under section 46 of the Companies Act, make distributions to its shareholders if so authorized pursuant to an existing legal obligation of the company or a court order or if the board of the company has authorized the distribution. However, a company may not make a distribution unless it reasonably appears that the company will satisfy the solvency and liquidity test immediately after the proposed distribution. The board of the company is required, by resolution, to acknowledge that it has applied the solvency and liquidity test and reasonably concludes that the company will satisfy the solvency and liquidity test after completing the proposed distribution.

[127] Once the board has adopted the resolution referred to above, the relevant distribution must be fully carried out within 120 business days. Should this not be the case, the board is required to once again consider the solvency and liquidity test and acknowledge that it has done so and reasonably concluded that the company will satisfy the solvency and liquidity test after completing the proposed distribution.

[128] Should the distribution take the form of incurrence of a debt or other obligation, the board is required to test the solvency and liquidity of the company at the time that the debt or obligation is to be incurred. The solvency and liquidity test will not apply to any subsequent action of the company in satisfaction of the debt or obligation.

[129] In the event that a company does not satisfy the solvency and liquidity test and is therefore unable to immediately satisfy a court order requiring the company to make a distribution, the company may apply to a court for an order varying the original order, and the court may make an order that:

- is just and equitable, having regard to the financial circumstances of the company; and
- ensures that the person to whom the company is required to make a payment in terms of the original order is paid at the earliest possible date compatible with the company satisfying its other financial obligations as they fall due and payable.

[130] A director may be liable for any loss, damage or costs sustained by the company as a direct or indirect consequence of his actions if he was present at the meeting or participated in the decision that approved the distribution and failed to vote against such resolution despite knowing that the distribution was contrary to section 46.

[131] Payments to shareholders need not be made out of 'profits' or any particular reserves of the company.

7 USE OF INCORPORATED JV OR UJV

[132] Corporate mergers and acquisitions often result in some form of a JV between the acquirer and target, going forward. In South Africa, a JV can be established and conducted either through a UJV, which is simply an agreement between the JV partners akin to a partnership, or through an incorporated JV, which is where the parties make use of a company and hold shares in that JV company.

[133] A UJV does not have a separate legal personality, whereas a JV company is a separate juristic person with its own assets and liabilities. A number of considerations will come into play in choosing the appropriate JV form, and these considerations are similar to what would be encountered in other jurisdictions. Incorporated JVs are the norm as they offer limited liability for the JV partners.

7.1 Advantages of a UJV as Against a JV Company

[134] UJVs are often entered into if, for commercial reasons, the parties wish to retain their independence and not pool their contributions or assets into a new entity. In a UJV, the parties would typically retain direct ownership and control of their respective assets or contracts that they contribute to the UJV's business.

[135] With a registered company, the assets are not owned by the shareholders but by the company. The shareholders have no rights to the assets of the company unless these are distributed by the company (as a distribution *in specie*, for instance) or sold by the company to its shareholders. Distributions have always been regulated by company law and are currently regulated by the Companies Act (section 46) which requires the company to comply with the solvency and liquidity test – therefore, if the company happens to be insolvent (even if only technically insolvent as opposed to commercially insolvent), no assets may be distributed to the shareholders, and these are 'trapped' in the company until it is wound up. Thus, with a UJV, the parties are not faced with these potential statutory hurdles in 'withdrawing' assets from the business – they can freely regulate these matters by agreement.

[136] A similar issue to the above is the question of sharing the income. Again, with a company, the shareholders do not have a right to the income received by the company – they only have a right to distributions (lawfully) declared by the company, which distributions must comply with various requirements of the Companies Act. There is also the requirement that a board resolution must be passed declaring the distribution. If the board refuses to declare a dividend, there is not much a shareholder can do other than to remove the director(s) (but then only if the shareholder happens to hold a majority of the shares and the director was, in fact, elected by a majority of the shareholders as opposed to being directly appointed – section 71(1) of the Companies Act) or apply to court for an order that the director is breaching his fiduciary duties to the company (which means the general body of shareholders as a whole in this context).

[137] A shareholder may also find itself in a situation where it does not reap the benefits of the company's profits if it happens to be the case that the company will not satisfy the solvency and liquidity test in the Companies Act pursuant to implementing the distribution. With a UJV, however, the income will typically flow into a separate bank account under the control of the parties, and there is no hindrance to this income being immediately on-paid to the parties – in most instances, after meeting the agreed budgeted expenses of the company. However, with this, there is still the risk that, in case of a dispute, the other party may not cooperate in transferring the funds out of the bank account.

[138] UJVs are not subject to the extensive regulation and administrative aspects contained in the Companies Act. One does not need to audit a separate legal entity. There are no filings of annual returns required, and no board committees are required to be appointed (certain companies are, in terms of the Companies Act, obliged to have audit committees and social and ethics committees. All public companies need to have audit committees unless their holding company has an audit committee that performs the same functions for the subsidiary. This entails having to have at least three independent non-executive directors. Large public and private companies that obtain a certain 'public interest score' in terms of the Companies Regulations also need to have social and ethics committees, which require non-executive directors and prescribed officers as members). Also, the incorporation of a company in the first place, which in itself involves costs, is not a concern in a UJV.

[139] Flowing from the point above is the fact that if there are changes in the percentages of participatory interest and/or changes in control of the UJV business, there is less of a chance that any of the complex takeover provisions or regulations of the Companies Act will apply than would be the case where shareholdings in a Regulated Company were to change (however, from a competition law approval perspective there is, largely, no difference).

[140] Director (and prescribed officer) liability is a major issue under the Companies Act. If a company were to be formed, that company must have directors (presumably, nominees of the respective shareholders), and those directors would be subject to all of the potential personal liability for breach of duty under the Companies Act. With a UJV, the business is conducted directly by the parties (being companies themselves), and one is not, at least directly, exposed to director liability. The director liability, if any, would be at JV partner level if a JV partner's director committed a breach. The so-called management committees set up by UJV agreements are not boards of directors and are thus not subject to the same governance regime as boards. (However, this could also be viewed as a disadvantage.)

[141] With a company, one faces the potential problem of deregistration. It is public knowledge that thousands of companies and close corporations have recently been subject to deregistration by the CIPC. While a deregistration can occur for relatively minor administrative oversights by a company (for instance, failure to file an annual return), the consequences of such deregistration are quite drastic. For instance, the assets of the company, by law, become the property of the state. It can be a costly exercise to reregister the company. There are no concerns of deregistrations in the context of UJVs.

[142] In the company law context, inter-company (or 'intra-group') financial assistance is quite extensively regulated and requires special resolutions of shareholders, solvency and liquidity and fairness and reasonableness (*see* section 45 of the Companies Act). Therefore, a shareholder which happens to be a holding entity (or, for that matter, in any way directly or indirectly controls the company) would have to comply with all these requirements before advancing a loan to the company, or providing a surety/guarantee for its benefit, which could potentially result in a delay depending on how many shareholders there are, etc. With a UJV, this is less of a concern.

[143] The dissolution of a UJV would typically be simpler and quicker. The contract is simply cancelled, and the parties retain their assets and go their separate ways (depending on whether they have, in terms of the agreement, retained sole ownership of the assets(s)). With a company, a formal winding-up in terms of the numerous procedures in the Companies Act needs to occur, which may be lengthy and costly depending on the extent of the company's operations. For this reason, UJVs tend to be most appropriate where the project is a one-off project (or of a limited duration) and relatively simple in its scope. However, it is not to say that the dissolution of a UJV is necessarily uncomplicated. Often, the agreement provides for a liquidator to be appointed and a liquidation process to be followed. But, there is greater room for contractual freedom in determining how the liquidation is to take place.

[144] There is a degree of publicity when dealing with a company in that the company's MOI and other company secretarial information must be filed at the CIPC and is available for public viewing. With UJVs, there are no such publicity requirements.

7.2 Advantages of a JV Company as Against a UJV

[145] The most important disadvantage of a UJV is that there is no benefit of limited liability, in that the parties will be personally liable for the debts incurred in the course of the UJV business. A UJV is simply a contract among the parties and is not a separate legal entity. This would not be the case if they were shareholders of a company (unless, of course, they bound themselves as sureties or guarantors of the company in favour of a third party or if a court were to 'pierce the corporate veil' and hold the shareholders liable for the company's debts or obligations, but this happens only under exceptional circumstances). The principal reason for using a company is the advantage of limited liability.

[146] Another aspect pertains to the saleability of parties' interests in the JV. Shares in companies can be sold fairly easily. But with a UJV, conceptually, the entry of new parties is more complicated. It could be possible, in law, to cede and assign a participatory interest in a UJV to a new party, but whether this works commercially is an entirely different question. Typically, the UJV would have to be terminated and an entirely new UJV established by contract, which, compared to the sale and purchase of a share in an already established and operational company, could potentially be far more lengthy and costly.

[147] The Companies Act contains a host of statutory shareholder protections and remedies that may be available to aggrieved parties, some of which offer highly useful protections against derelict directors or oppressive majority shareholders. These remedies would, of course, not be available outside the company law context, and in a UJV, the parties would have to rely solely on their contractual rights and remedies as well as those in common law if any, which might not always be as extensive as those in the Companies Act. However, it is possible to contractually agree on similar remedies to those in the Companies Act.

[148] If the UJV becomes financially distressed, it will not be able to use the benefits of the business rescue mechanisms in the Companies Act, which essentially provide for a temporary moratorium on claims against a company in order to allow it to return to profitability.

[149] A risk in relation to UJVs is that they may be characterized by a court as a partnership (in the legal-technical sense) if they meet the essential elements of a partnership in law. The risk is that it might not help the parties to expressly state in their UJV agreement that their relationship is not a partnership because the real question is whether, in fact and in law, there is a partnership. With this, some considerable potential disadvantages follow:

- The partners have a mutual mandate and can bind each other's credit (although this can be restricted in a UJV agreement).
- Co-partners can be held vicariously liable in delict (i.e., for damages) caused by a partner to a third party, as well as in criminal law.
- After termination of a partnership (but before final liquidation), the ex-partners become jointly and severally liable for partnership debts that existed at the time of the termination. This means that a creditor can claim the full amount from one partner, and that partner would then have to recover the pro rata shares from the other partners.

7.3 Setting up of a JV Company

[150] The vehicle that is typically used in South Africa for purposes of an incorporated JV is the private company envisaged in the Companies Act. There are two ways of obtaining a private company in South Africa: either one incorporates and registers a company 'from scratch' by lodging an MOI in respect of the company (which is negotiated and adopted by the shareholders), or one makes use of a shelf company that is already incorporated.

[151] Shelf companies do not have any assets or liabilities and can be readily purchased and 'reformatted' in order to bring the shareholding and directorship in line with the investors' requirements. The benefit of a shelf company is that one need not wait for the company to be registered at the CIPC. It is already registered, and the main steps to be taken thereafter are as follows:

- Issue shares to the JV parties.
- The resignation of the existing director.
- The election of the JV parties' desired directors.
- The negotiation and adoption of a customized MOI which replaces the existing generic or standard MOI once it is filed at the CIPC.

[152] The JV company needs to be capitalized. This can be done by way of equity (share capital) or debt (shareholder loans), or a combination of both. The use of one method or the other is often driven by tax and exchange control considerations. South African company law does not have any thin capitalization rules, which means that a domestic resident company can effectively have a shareholding of ZAR1 of equity and unlimited borrowings (although the tax implications of this must be considered). The closest the company law comes to regulating 'thin capitalization' is indirectly through:

- the solvency and liquidity test and the rules on reckless/commercially insolvent trading, which provisions may have implications for what a company may do when it is thinly capitalized but do not outright prohibit a state of affairs where a company's debt substantially outweighs its share capital; and
- the requirement that shares be issued for 'adequate consideration' as determined by the board, in terms of section 40 of the Companies Act.

[153] The constitutional documents of a company will contain a number of provisions relating to the relationship between the shareholders as well as in respect of the JV company itself. These include, among others: percentages of shareholding, board representation, disposal of shares and exit from the structure, which matters or transactions are reserved for shareholder approval, funding arrangements, BEE undertakings, if any, etc. In order to achieve BEE targets, BEE shareholders must be 'locked-in' and undertake not to do anything that would jeopardize the JV company's BEE status.

8 EXCHANGE CONTROL

[154] South Africa is subject to exchange control regulations which imply that foreign investments and the repatriation of funds are regulated and require the approval of the South African Reserve Bank (SARB). SARB has delegated much of its power and authority to so-called authorized dealers (essentially banks and other institutions licensed to undertake exchange control functions and grant approvals under exchange control). Despite recent litigation concerning 'exit levies' on private emigrants' wealth that ended up in the Constitutional Court in 2015, exchange control remains very much part of the South African business law and merger landscape. It is anticipated that the exchange control regulatory landscape is to undergo a substantial overhaul in the near future, and therefore developments in this regard need to be monitored.

[155] The present position is that the exchange control authorities have a wide discretion that is exercised in accordance with the Exchange Control Regulations, 1961 (including the various orders and rules issued under the said Regulations). Prior to 29 July 2016, the Exchange Control Rulings, which had been in place since 2005 and were drafted in line with the policy guidelines laid down by the Minister of Finance, had provided further guidance on the discretion of exchange control. In the 2016 Budget Speech, the Minister of Finance announced that simplified manuals and guideline documents would be published by the SARB's Financial

Surveillance Department (FinSurv). On 29 July 2016, FinSurv released Exchange Control Circular No. 7/2016 (Circular No. 7/2016), in terms of which the Exchange Control Rulings were replaced by the Currency and Exchanges Manual for Authorised Dealers (Authorised Dealers Manual) and the Currency and Exchanges Manual for Authorised Dealers in foreign exchange with limited authority. The Exchange Control Manual that had been in place was replaced with two guideline documents, namely the Currency and Exchanges Guidelines for Individuals and the Currency and Exchanges Guidelines for Business Entities. The manuals and guideline documents took effect on 1 August 2016. The aim of the manuals is to assist dealers, their customers and other interested parties by providing a general understanding of the purpose, scope and operation of the exchange control system in the Republic and other countries in the Common Monetary Area jurisdictions. In general, the Exchange Control Rulings and Exchange Control Manuals were published since 1990 and were amended from time to time through the issuance of exchange control circulars by FinSurv.

[156] All applications for exchange control approval must be made through an authorized dealer. In respect of smaller transactions, an authorized dealer is generally prepared to grant the requisite approval itself; however, when more substantial transactions are involved, it is quite usual that an authorized dealer would rather refer the matter to the SARB for its approval. An authorized dealer would then facilitate the application to the SARB. In practice, the process of obtaining exchange control approval is relatively fast if all requisite documents are properly submitted. The exchange control system has been gradually liberalized over the past few years in South Africa, and it is the stated intention of the National Treasury that the gradual liberalization and deregulation of exchange control will continue. Most (but not all) of the exchange control policies and regulations are focused on the exchange control transactions of South African residents (i.e., outward transactions). It is important to keep in mind that the interpretation of the Exchange Control Regulations and Manuals (previously Rulings), on which the exchange control system is based, is largely subject to the policies of the SARB, the National Treasury and the particular authorized dealer handling the exchange control application.

[157] Generally speaking, a non-resident investor may freely invest in South Africa, provided that suitable documentary evidence is available in order to ensure that the transactions are concluded at arm's length, at fair market value and are financed in an approved (by exchange control authorities) manner. Non-resident investors seeking to invest in, and introduce funds into, South Africa may either purchase South African currency or borrow funds locally. The use of these mediums is regulated by exchange control law, and approval will be dependent on the nature of the investment. Exchange control authorities will generally permit either loan capital or equity to be introduced into the country via the South African Rand.

[158] A non-resident has a great degree of flexibility in the way in which it funds a South African investee company's operations. Consideration should be given to possible adverse tax implications if the amount of interest-bearing debt of the resident, or the rate of interest payable, is too high. Although exchange control does not insist on a specific shareholder debt-to-equity ratio, the introduction of loan funding, its repayment, as well as the interest rate charged nevertheless remain subject to prior approval by the authorities.

[159] The repatriation of funds is also regulated by exchange control. The proceeds from the sale of assets owned by a non-resident (e.g., the shares of a non-resident investor in a local company) are remittable to the non-resident. Dividends declared by non-listed South African companies are remittable to non-resident shareholders in proportion to the percentage shareholding of the non-resident shareholder in question. Certificated securities of any nature in which there is a non-resident interest of any nature whatsoever must be endorsed 'Non-Resident'. There are also other exchange approval measures that might be applicable when an investor invests in South Africa.

[160] With regard to loans, prior approval from exchange control authorities for both the advance of loan capital from outside of South Africa and the repatriation of funds brought into South Africa as loan capital is required. Such exchange control approval can, but does not always, provide that the loan in question can be repaid only out of the profits of the company. Agreements whereby a South African company is obliged to pay royalties, licence or patent fees to a non-resident are subject to approval by the Department of Trade and Industry where the products in question are manufactured locally and by exchange control authorities in all other cases. Such royalty payments will also have to be substantiated by an auditor's report confirming the basis of calculation and that it is in terms of an approved agreement. According to the Authorised Dealers Manual, the minimum payments, advance payments and down payments of royalties are permissible, provided that the advance payments and down payments are recoupable from future royalties or fees payable.

[161] Generally, authorized dealers may approve applications by residents to make payments for services rendered by non-residents, provided that the said fees are not determined by reference to turnover, income, sales or purchases.

[162] The following high-level tax consequences may have an impact on the mechanisms used to inject or remove cash from the South African subsidiary, by a foreign investor/shareholder. If the subsidiary is funded by way of interest-bearing loan from its shareholder/an offshore group company, it is noted that the tax deductibility of interest is currently limited in terms of the provisions of section 31 of the Income Tax Act which requires:

- from a transfer pricing perspective, the interest rate must be at arm's length; and
- from a thin capitalization perspective, a shareholder/group loan (financial assistance) should be based on arm's-length principles. South Africa no longer has a safe harbour debt-to-equity ratio of 3:1.

On 28 October 2016, SARS released a notice in the Government Gazette in terms of which persons who enter into transactions under section 31 of the Income Tax Act will be required to keep specified records, books of account or documents in respect of the structure of the taxpayer's operations and in respect of transactions to which the provisions of section 31 of the Income Tax Act apply.

Effective 1 January 2015, the interest that is paid to a non-resident may be subject to a 15% withholding tax. The resident paying the interest is required to withhold the tax and pay it to SARS. South Africa's withholding tax on interest may be reduced by the provisions of an applicable Double Taxation Agreement (DTA). Dividends paid to a non-resident may be subject to a 20% withholding tax. South Africa's withholding tax on dividends may be reduced by the provisions of an applicable DTA. A subsidiary may be able to justify the payment of management fees and like payments to its offshore holding/group company. These are also subject to South Africa's transfer pricing provisions and Exchange Control Regulations. Management fees are not subject to withholding tax in South Africa; however, under certain circumstances, the payment of management fees for certain services will constitute a reportable arrangement, which must be reported to SARS in terms of section 35 of the Tax Administration Act 28 of 2011. A subsidiary may be able to justify the payment of royalties and like payments to its offshore holding company. There are certain anti-avoidance rules as to the deductibility of royalties. These are also subject to South Africa's transfer pricing provisions and South Africa's Exchange Control Regulations. Royalties paid to non-residents, which do not carry on business through a permanent establishment in South Africa, are currently subject to a 15% withholding tax. However, this may be reduced by the provisions of an applicable DTA.

9 TAX

[163] Direct taxes are taxes which are imposed on persons (individuals, trusts, deceased estates, insolvent estates, companies and close corporations). The direct taxes imposed in South Africa are: income tax, capital gains tax (CGT), dividends tax, donations tax and estate duty. Indirect taxes are taxes which are levied on transactions rather than on persons. The indirect taxes imposed in South Africa include value added tax (VAT), securities transfer tax (STT) (previously stamp duty/uncertificated securities tax), the mining royalty, transfer duty, customs and excise duty and the carbon tax which came into effect in June 2019.

[164] Taxes on income and profits are levied by the national government in terms of the Income Tax Act. The Income Tax Act is administered by the Commissioner of SARS. The Income Tax Act contains provisions for the levying of four different types of tax, namely: normal tax (on income and on capital gains), dividends tax, donations tax and various withholding taxes. Income tax is an annual tax and represents a levy imposed on all persons who have a taxable income. The tax is calculated by applying predetermined rates to the taxable income of a person. For this purpose, a distinction is drawn between natural persons (individuals), juristic persons (such as companies and close corporations) and trusts.

[165] As from 2001, South Africa moved from a source-based income tax system to a residence-based income tax system. Residents (juristic and non-juristic) are (subject to certain exclusions) taxed on their worldwide income, irrespective of where the income is earned. However, the source continues to be relevant since persons who are not resident in South Africa are subject to tax in South Africa on all income which is from a South African source. South African residents are also taxed on the net income of a controlled foreign company (CFC) (subject to certain exclusions) in proportion to their participation rights in that CFC. A CFC is any foreign company where more than 50% of the total participation rights or voting rights are held by South African residents. Further, South Africa has entered into DTAs with various countries, which are aimed at regulating the taxation of income which is earned in one state and subject to tax in the other state. The principal objective of the DTA is to avoid double taxation. Where, however, the same income is taxed twice, any foreign taxes that are required to be paid by South African residents in respect of the foreign income would be credited against any South African tax payable on that foreign income. The credit cannot exceed the South African tax liability arising on such foreign income (determined as a ratio of total foreign taxable income to total South African income). Any excess may be carried forward for a period of up to seven years and set off against South African tax payable on foreign income in the future. In resolving tax conflicts, treaties often use the source of income as the basis for the provisions contained in the treaty.

[166] A juristic person (companies and close corporations) and a trust will be a resident of South Africa if it is incorporated, established or formed in South Africa or if it has its place of effective management in South Africa. Currently, the term 'effective management' refers to the place where the company is managed on a regular day-to-day basis by the executive directors or senior managers of the company, irrespective of where the overriding or central management and control are exercised, or where the board of directors meets. It is effectively the place of execution and implementation of the company's policy and strategic decisions. In terms of SARS' interpretation note of 2015, a company's place of effective management is the place where key management and commercial decisions that are necessary for the conduct of its business as a whole are in substance made. This approach is consistent with the Organisation for Economic Co-operation and Development's commentary on the term 'place of effective management'. A company may have more than one place of management, but it can only have one place of effective management at any one time. There are normally multiple facts that need to be taken into account, often involving multiple locations, and from those facts and locations, it is, therefore, necessary to determine a single dominant place where effective management is located. Definitive rules cannot be laid down in determining the place of effective management, and all relevant facts and circumstances must be examined on a case-by-case basis. The place of effective management test is one of substance over form. It, therefore, requires a determination of those persons in a company who actually 'call the shots' and exercise 'realistic positive management'.

[167] CGT is not a separate tax but is 'normal tax' payable on the taxable portion of a capital gain. CGT is a tax levied on capital gains arising from the disposal of assets. A capital gain arises when the proceeds from the disposal of an asset exceed the base cost of that asset. South African resident companies and individuals would be subject to CGT on the disposal of their worldwide assets subject to the applicability of a DTA. Should a taxpayer realize a net capital loss during the year of assessment, the loss cannot be used to reduce other taxable income but is carried forward to be offset against future capital gains. Non-residents are liable for CGT on the following assets:

- immovable property situated in South Africa (e.g., land and buildings);
- any right or interest in immovable property in South Africa (e.g., a long-term lease);
- an equity share in a company or ownership or the right of ownership or a vested interest in assets of a trust where 80% or more of the market value (at the time of disposal of that share or interest) is attributable to immovable property in South Africa that is held otherwise than as trading stock and, in the case of a company or other entity, the non-resident holds directly or indirectly 20% or more of the equity shares or ownership in the company; and
- assets of a permanent establishment (e.g., a branch of a foreign company) situated in South Africa.

As noted above, relief from double taxation may be granted by an applicable DTA.

CGT will not be levied where a transaction meets the requirements of the corporate rollover relief provisions, which are dealt with in sections 41–47 of the Income Tax Act. These transactions are quite commonly used where a company undertakes a restructuring of its internal operations. Corporate rollover relief will apply to certain qualifying transactions, including asset-for-share transactions, substitutive share-for-share transactions, amalgamation transactions, intra-group transactions, unbundling transactions and transactions relating to liquidation, winding-up and deregistration of a company. Where a transaction qualifies for the rollover relief, the capital gain will be 'rolled-over' as it were, so that CGT will only be payable when a person subsequently disposes of the asset. Rollover relief is generally only available to companies but is also available to natural persons in very limited circumstances.

[168] South Africa introduced a dividends tax in 2012, which replaced the secondary tax on companies and is levied at the rate of 20% of any dividend paid by a company. The tax is levied in respect of dividends paid by resident companies and certain foreign companies that are listed locally. The person liable for the tax is the beneficial owner of the dividend. However, where the dividend is a dividend *in specie*, the company paying the dividend will be liable. Generally, the company paying the dividend must withhold the dividends tax and pay it over to SARS. Dividends paid to resident companies are exempt, but not dividends paid to foreign companies. However, where a DTA applies, the rate of dividends tax to be withheld can potentially be reduced.

[169] Donations tax is levied at a flat rate of 20% on the value of property donated and is payable by the donor. Donations tax is not applicable to donations made by non-residents, even if South African assets are being donated. South African resident individuals are allowed to make exempt donations up to ZAR100 000 per year of assessment. Donations to an approved PBO are exempt from donations tax, subject to certain conditions. Donations to certain tax-exempt organizations may also, in certain circumstances, qualify as a deduction from the donor's taxable income. It should be noted that where any property has been disposed of for a consideration, which, in the opinion of the Commissioner, is not an adequate consideration, that property is treated as having been disposed of under a donation.

[170] VAT is largely directed at the domestic consumption of goods and services and at goods and services imported into South Africa. The tax is designed to be paid mainly by the ultimate consumer or purchaser in South Africa. VAT is levied at a standard rate of 15%. Most business transactions carried out in South Africa are subject to VAT. The tax is collected by businesses that are registered as vendors with SARS. Vendors charge VAT on supplies made (output tax) and deduct VAT on expenses (input VAT). The output tax collected may be reduced by the input tax paid. The net amount is payable to or refundable by SARS. Any entity is required to register as a vendor for VAT purposes where it carries on an enterprise in South Africa, in the course of which its turnover exceeds ZAR1 m per annum. From 1 April 2014, persons who supply certain electronic services, as defined by regulation, from an export country to South African residents who have a business address, residential address or postal address in South Africa have to also register for VAT if their turnover from the rendering of these services exceeds ZAR50 000 in any given month. It should be noted that services rendered by a vendor to a non-resident generally qualify for zero-rating (i.e., the levying of VAT at 0%), provided that the non-resident is not in South Africa at the time the services are rendered.

[171] STT is payable at a rate of 0.25% of the consideration or market value (whichever is higher) on the transfer of any security issued by a South African company or a member's interest in a South African close corporation, or a share in any foreign company listed on a South African stock exchange, subject to certain exemptions. The cession of dividend rights will also be subject to STT. STT is also payable on the cancellation or redemption of a security where the issuer is not being wound up.

[172] The Carbon Tax Act, No. 15 of 2019, came into effect on 1 June 2019. Simply put, carbon tax is imposed on the carbon dioxide equivalent of greenhouse gas emissions where certain thresholds are exceeded and is intended to encourage the reduction of greenhouse gas emissions in South Africa and to ensure that South Africa meets its commitments under the Paris Agreement. With regard to calculating carbon tax liability, the first phase has a carbon tax rate of ZAR120 per ton of carbon dioxide equivalent emissions. This rate will increase annually by inflation plus 2% until 2022, and annually by inflation thereafter. Significant industry-specific tax-free emissions allowances ranging from 60% to 95% will result in a modest net carbon tax rate ranging from ZAR6 to ZAR48 per ton of carbon dioxide equivalent emissions to provide current emitters time to transition their operations to cleaner technologies through investments in energy efficiency, renewables, and other low-carbon measures.

10 COMPETITION LAW AND MERGER CONTROL

[173] South Africa has a very modern and developed system of competition law which essentially regulates two broad aspects: merger control and prohibited practices. The commercial activities which are prohibited under the Competition Act are concerned with conduct relating to a firm's dealings with its competitors (horizontal relationship), with its customers and suppliers (vertical relationship), and unilateral conduct by a dominant firm (abuse of dominance). A number of competition law-related measures and dispensations were introduced during the nationwide lockdown in South Africa during March/April 2020 because of COVID-19 pandemic; however, it is anticipated that these are to be of a temporary nature to address the very specific circumstances and concerns brought about by the pandemic in relation to pricing and competition in the market.

[174] With regard to horizontal prohibited practices, section 4 of the Competition Act prohibits certain conduct arising out of an agreement between, or concerted practice by, firms which compete against each other. Outright prohibited practices between firms in a horizontal relationship consist of an agreement, practice or decision between competitors that involves:

- fixing prices or other trading conditions;
- dividing markets by allocating customers, suppliers, territories or specific types of goods or services; or
- collusive tendering.

Potentially prohibited practices between firms in a horizontal relationship consist of an agreement, practice or decision that has the effect of substantially preventing or lessening competition in the relevant market unless pro-competitive benefits are attributable to and outweigh the anticompetitive effect. With regard to vertical prohibited practices, section 5 of the Competition Act prohibits conduct arising out of the interaction between a firm and its customers or suppliers. It is prohibited for a firm to engage in the practice of minimum resale price maintenance. This means that a firm may not prohibit a customer from reselling its product at a price below the minimum level set by that firm. However, the Competition Act provides that a minimum resale price may be recommended. Potentially prohibited practices between firms in a vertical relationship consist of an agreement that has the effect of substantially preventing or lessening competition unless pro-competitive benefits are attributable to and outweigh the anticompetitive effect. An example of such conduct is an exclusive arrangement between a supplier and customer in respect of supply or purchase.

[175] Unilateral conduct by a dominant firm, which is regulated by sections 7, 8 and 9 of the Competition Act, relates to actions that constitute an abuse of a firm's dominant position in a relevant market. Dominance is construed as market power which allows a firm to control prices, exclude competition or behave to an appreciable extent independently of its competitors, customers and suppliers.

[176] Merger control is concerned with the regulation of large mergers and acquisitions in South Africa. The Competition Act establishes three categories of mergers which are determined with reference to the turnover or assets (whichever is the higher) of the acquiring firm and the target firm. 'Merger' under the Competition Act encompasses any form of change of control of a firm, and it is irrelevant whether the corporate merger or acquisition took the form of a sale of shares, sale of business, scheme of arrangement, statutory amalgamation, JV arrangement or otherwise.

[177] A small merger occurs where the combined assets or turnover of the acquiring firm and the target firm are below ZAR600 m, or the target firm's assets or turnover are below ZAR100 m. An intermediate merger occurs where the combined assets or turnover of the acquiring firm and the target firm equal or exceed ZAR600 m and the target firm's assets or turnover equal or exceed ZAR100 m. A large merger occurs where the combined assets or turnover of the acquiring firm and the target firm equal or exceed ZAR6.6 bn and the target firm's assets or turnover equal or exceed ZAR190 m. For purposes of calculating the thresholds, the entire acquirer group is taken into account. In relation to the target firm, the firm over which control is transferred, together with all firms controlled by such transferred firm, is taken into account. The parties to an intermediate or large merger may not implement the merger without the approval of the competition authorities.

11 LABOUR LAW AND EMPLOYMENT EQUITY CONSIDERATIONS

[178] The protection of employees' rights is a key feature of South African law and has an important effect in the context of corporate mergers and acquisitions. Under section 197 of the Labour Relations Act 66 of 1995 (LRA), if a transfer of a business takes place, unless otherwise agreed as described below:

- the new employer (purchaser) is automatically substituted in the place of the old employer (seller) in respect of all contracts of employment in existence immediately before the date of transfer;
- all the rights and obligations between the old employer and an employee at the time of the transfer continue in force as if they had been rights and obligations between the new employer and the employee;
- anything done before the transfer by or in relation to the old employer, including the dismissal of an employee or the commission of an unfair labour practice or act of unfair discrimination, is considered to have been done by or in relation to the new employer; and
- the transfer does not interrupt an employee's continuity of employment, and an employee's contract of employment continues with the new employer as if with the old employer.

It is accepted that a sale of shares in a company (and therefore a change in its owners), as opposed to a sale of its business, does not amount to a 'transfer of business' under section 197.

[179] The new employer is deemed to have complied with the above if that employer employs transferred employees on terms and conditions that are on the whole not less favourable to the employees than those on which they were employed by the old employer.

[180] An agreement to exclude the application of the automatic transfer of employees must be in writing and concluded between the old employer, the new employer, or the old and new employers acting jointly, on the one hand, and the appropriate person or body that represents the old employer's employees (e.g., trade union), on the other hand. In any negotiations to conclude such a tripartite agreement, the employers must disclose to the employees/trade union all relevant information that will allow it to engage effectively in the negotiations.

[181] The old employer must agree with the new employer to a valuation as at the date of transfer of the leave pay accrued to the transferred employees of the old employer; the severance pay that would have been payable to the transferred employees of the old employer in the event of a dismissal by reason of the employer's operational requirements; and any other payments that have accrued to the transferred employees but have not been paid to employees of the old employer. An agreement must be concluded that specifies:

- which employer is liable for paying any amount referred to above, and in the case of the apportionment of liability between them, the terms of that apportionment; and
- what provision has been made for any payment contemplated above if any employee becomes entitled to receive a payment.

[182] Transfers of employees from insolvent businesses are treated somewhat differently, under section 197A of the LRA. Section 197A applies to a transfer of a business if the old employer is insolvent or if a scheme of arrangement or compromise is being entered into to avoid winding-up or sequestration for reasons of insolvency. In such a case, the new employer is automatically substituted in the place of the old employer in all contracts of employment in existence immediately before the old employer's provisional winding-up or sequestration, but all the rights and obligations between the old employer and each employee at the time of the transfer remain rights and obligations between the old employer and each employee. Further, anything done before the transfer by the old employer in respect of each employee is considered to have been done by the old employer, not the new employer. This section, which is substantially less onerous insofar as the purchaser is concerned, is aimed at encouraging and facilitating the rescue of insolvent businesses through mergers, schemes and business transfers.

[183] South Africa has an extensive employment equity law regime. Any 'designated employer' must take affirmative action measures designed to ensure that suitably qualified people from designated groups have equal employment opportunities and are equitably represented in all occupational categories and levels in the workforce of a designated employer. A designated employer is one who employs fifty or more employees or less than fifty employees but has a total annual turnover that is equal to or above ZAR10 m per annum. The ratios apply to designated groups, meaning citizens of South Africa who are black people, women and people with disabilities. The ratio does not apply to local personnel versus foreign secondees.

[184] Foreign secondees are subject to the South African immigration laws if seconded to any employer in South Africa. They require a work permit. Work permits are subject to a skills shortage of South African qualified citizens and are limited in duration. In terms of proposed legislation to be implemented in the near future, employers must also satisfy themselves that there are no other persons in South

Africa with suitable skills to fill a vacancy before recruiting a foreign national or before a foreign national is employed as a secondee and must in addition prepare and submit a skills transfer plan in respect of any position in which a foreign national is employed.

12 USE OF FOREIGN JURISDICTION CLAUSES IN COMMERCIAL CONTRACTS/JV AGREEMENTS

[185] To the extent that a corporate merger or acquisition involves foreign parties, South Africa's private international law or 'conflict of laws' may come into play. It is a fairly well-developed area of law in South Africa. Clauses providing for a contract to be governed, arbitrated or litigated under a foreign law are enforceable in South Africa. A South African court tasked to decide upon a dispute between parties in terms of such a clause may require a litigant to adduce evidence as to the content of the applicable foreign law. South African legislation specifically provides that any court may take 'judicial notice' of the law of a foreign state where the law can be ascertained readily and with sufficient certainty. A court may even consider the applicability of foreign law without it having been pleaded specifically if it is in the interests of justice to do so and provided the parties have been given an opportunity to address the court on the issue. Parties may, for example, call an expert witness to testify as to the substance of a legal rule which is in issue at the proceedings concerned. The expert would need to be sufficiently qualified to prove the relevant law, and his/her role would be to inform the judge, not to decide the issue. Expert evidence that is contradictory may be rejected out of hand, or the court may examine the witness' sources in order to reach its own conclusions about the foreign law. The court must be placed in a position to determine the foreign law with sufficient certainty.

[186] It is not possible for parties to exclude entirely the jurisdiction of a South African court by their own agreement where that court would otherwise have had jurisdiction over the matter. The Supreme Court of Appeal has provided some guidance on this issue and indicated that a party wishing to invoke the protection of a foreign jurisdiction or arbitration clause would have to do so by way of a special or dilatory plea seeking a stay of the proceedings. The court would then be called upon to exercise its discretion whether or not to enforce the clause in question, taking into account all the relevant facts and circumstances. The court's discretion lies in deciding whether or not the exercise of its jurisdiction should be stayed pending the outcome of foreign proceedings or arbitration.

[187] The recently enacted International Arbitration Act 15 of 2017 (IA Act) has modernized the law in South Africa concerning international arbitration and foreign arbitral awards. The objects of the IA Act are to facilitate the use of arbitration as a method of resolving international commercial disputes, to adopt the Model Law (i.e., the Model Law on International Commercial Arbitration, as adopted by the United Nations Commission on International Trade Law) for use in international commercial disputes, to facilitate the recognition and enforcement of certain arbitration agreements and arbitral awards, and to give effect to the obligations of South Africa under the Convention on the Recognition and Enforcement of Foreign Arbitral Awards (1958). In terms of the IA Act, subject to section 18 thereof, an arbitration agreement and a foreign arbitral award must be recognized and enforced in South Africa as required by the said Convention. A foreign arbitral award is binding between the parties to that foreign arbitral award and may be relied upon by those parties by way of defence, set-off or otherwise in any legal proceedings. A foreign arbitral award must, on application, be made an order of court and may then be enforced in the same manner as any judgment or order of the court, subject to the provisions of section 18. In terms of section 18 of the IA Act, a court may only refuse to recognize or enforce a foreign arbitral award if:

(a) the court finds that:
  (i) a reference to arbitration of the subject matter of the dispute is not permissible under the law of the Republic; or
  (ii) the recognition or enforcement of the award is contrary to the public policy of the Republic; or
(b) the party against whom the award is invoked proves to the satisfaction of the court that:
  (i) a party to the arbitration agreement had no capacity to contract under the law applicable to that party;
  (ii) the arbitration agreement is invalid under the law to which the parties have subjected it, or where the parties have not subjected it to any law, the arbitration agreement is invalid under the law of the country in which the award was made;
  (iii) he or she did not receive the required notice regarding the appointment of the arbitrator or of the arbitration proceedings or was otherwise not able to present his or her case;
  (iv) the award deals with a dispute not contemplated by, or not falling within the terms of the reference to arbitration, or contains decisions on matters beyond the scope of the reference to arbitration;
  (v) the constitution of the arbitration tribunal or the arbitration procedure was not in accordance with the relevant arbitration agreement or, if the agreement does not provide for such matters, with the law of the country in which the arbitration took place; or
  (vi) the award is not yet binding on the parties, or has been set aside or suspended by a competent authority of the country in which, or under the law of which, the award was made.

13 PROPERTY LAW/REAL ESTATE CONSIDERATIONS

[188] The transfer of ownership in land is effected by registration in a deeds registry in accordance with the provision of the Deeds Registries Act 47 of 1937. South

Africa boasts a sophisticated and efficient system of land registration. The system is one of registration of title as opposed to a system of registration of deeds as is found in many western countries. Although the system of registration may be described as a negative system, that is, one in which the state does not guarantee title, disputes as to the validity of title are few and far between. The South African system of registration effectively provides the registered owner of land with the security of title. This security of title is the result of the respective responsibilities carried by professional land surveyors (under the authority of a Surveyor-general), the deeds registries established throughout South Africa (each under the authority of a Registrar of Deeds, with a Chief Registrar of Deeds exercising authority on a national basis) and an independent attorneys' profession. In the latter case, the preparation and execution of deeds require the services of an attorney in professional practice who has passed a specialist examination in the law and practice of conveyancing and has been admitted to practise as a conveyancer by the High Court of South Africa.

[189] While the common law ownership of land includes the ownership of all fixed improvements erected on the land, South African law also recognizes separate ownership of buildings or parts of a building. Such ownership is regulated by the Sectional Titles Act 95 of 1986. Sectional title ownership is also registered in a deeds registry. Statutory rights in land are also provided for in the Share Blocks Control Act 59 of 1980. This form of tenure entitles the holder of shares in a share block company to the use and enjoyment of land owned or leased by the share block company. This form of tenure is not registered in a deeds registry and the rights attaching thereto are protected by the Share Blocks Control Act. South African law recognizes various limited rights in land, the most common of which is the relationship of landlord and tenant. Leases are capable of registration in the deeds registry and, in such instances, afford the tenant greater rights than in the case of an unregistered lease.

[190] Rights to minerals in South Africa are regulated by the Mineral and Petroleum Resources Development Act 28 of 2002. The Act makes provision for equitable access to and development of the nation's mineral and petroleum resources and recognizes the internationally accepted right of the state to exercise sovereignty over all the mineral and petroleum resources within the Republic. Provision is made in the Act for guaranteeing security of tenure in respect of prospecting and mining operations.

[191] In the case of the acquisition of land or any real right in land (as well as certain transactions involving companies, trusts and other legal entities that own residential property), a transfer duty is, subject to certain exceptions, payable prior to registration in the deeds registry. This duty generally amounts to a percentage of the value of the land or right, calculated on a sliding scale, and applies equally to both individuals and companies or trusts. Certain transactions are exempt from transfer duty. This is regulated by the Transfer Duty Act 40 of 1949. In terms of the VAT Act, VAT (currently at the rate of 15%) is payable, subject to certain exemptions, on the supply by a vendor of goods or services supplied by him in the course of an enterprise. 'Goods' include fixed property and any real right in fixed property. Certain transactions relating to fixed property are subject to VAT at a rate of 0%. The acquisition of land in terms of a transaction that is subject to VAT is exempt from transfer duty.

14 WIND-UP/DISSOLUTION OF COMPANIES

[192] The exit from a JV/investee company may require its winding-up. There are three possible routes which may be followed in order to dissolve a company voluntarily:

(1) A voluntary creditors' winding-up (where the company is insolvent).
(2) A voluntary members' winding-up (where the company is solvent and able to pay its debts).
(3) A deregistration of the company on application to the CIPC, which is not a winding-up.

[193] Both forms of voluntary winding-up are initiated by the shareholders of the company by way of a special resolution (i.e., at least a 75% vote). The terminology 'creditors' voluntary winding-up' is often misleading because it suggests that a creditor initiates the winding-up, but this is not so from a legal perspective. It is still initiated by way of the passing and filing of a special resolution of shareholders; it is only after it is so initiated that the creditors 'control' the process going forward in that they control the appointment of the liquidator, and the liquidator must follow their instructions. Where the company being wound up is unable to pay its debts, the persons who are mainly interested are the creditors, and the shareholders have no real interest in the winding-up. Accordingly, where the company is unable to pay its debts, the winding-up is controlled by the creditors, who appoint the liquidator. The essential feature of a members' voluntary winding-up is the requirement that either security has been furnished to the satisfaction of the Master of the High Court for the payment of the company's debts or the Master has dispensed with such security because the company has no debts. Because the creditors' interests, if any, are thus secured, the liquidator exercises his powers subject to the directions of the shareholders. In the case of a creditors' voluntary winding-up, however, because no such security is furnished or dispensed with, the liquidator exercises his powers subject to the directions of the creditors.

[194] In a members' voluntary winding-up, a liquidator is appointed, and he simply settles all outstanding debts of the company after realizing/liquidating its assets and resources. However, with creditors' voluntary winding-up, the creditors submit proof of claims to the liquidator, and the liquidator settles their claims in accordance with the rankings of such creditors' claims.

[195] The Companies Act contains a mechanism whereby the board of a company may apply to the CIPC to simply deregister the company. The company is then still dissolved, and there is no need for a winding-up process. This option may be explored if the company is essentially dormant or is a shell. Section 82(3)(b)(ii) of the Companies Act allows the CIPC to deregister a company if the CIPC has received a request in the prescribed manner and form and has determined that the company has ceased to carry on business and has no assets or, because of the inadequacy of its assets, there is no reasonable probability of the company being liquidated/wound up. The CIPC exercises a discretion and will request appropriate affidavits from the company's directors as to the company's financial position.

15 FUTURE DEVELOPMENTS

[196] The majority of the bilateral investment treaties (BITs) South Africa concluded with countries it has trade and investment relationships with are near completion or are in the process of being terminated by the South African government (pursuant to the relevant BIT terms), as the intention is for South Africa to, in future, regulate the protection of foreign investments by means of national legislation in the form of the Protection of Investment Act 2015 (Investment Act) signed into law in December 2015. The commencement date of this Act was 13 July 2018. The stated object of the Investment Act is to: (a) protect investment in accordance with and subject to the Constitution in a manner which balances the public interest and the rights and obligations of investors; (b) affirm the Republic's sovereign right to regulate investments in the public interest; and (c) confirm the Bill of Rights in the Constitution and the laws that apply to all investors and their investments in the Republic.

[197] The Investment Act obliges the government to ensure administrative, legislative and judicial processes do not operate in a manner that is arbitrary or that denies administrative and procedural justice to investors in respect of their investments as provided for in the Constitution and applicable legislation. Administrative decision-making processes must include the right to be given written reasons and administrative review of the decision consistent with the Constitution and applicable legislation. Investors must, in respect of their investments, have access to government-held information in a timely fashion and consistent with the Constitution and applicable legislation. All investments must be established in compliance with the laws of the Republic. Foreign investors and their investments must not be treated less favourably than South African investors in like circumstances. For this purpose, 'like circumstances' means the requirement for an overall examination of the merits of the case by taking into account all the terms of a foreign investment.

www.ingramcontent.com/pod-product-compliance
Lightning Source LLC
Chambersburg PA
CBHW071400230926
51846CB00002B/605
9789403525983